CORRUPTION
—— IN THE ——
DIVISION
—— OF ——
CORRECTIONS

Inspired by a True Story

CHINYERE UDEH

All Martha's Writers L.L.C.
Williston St. Baltimore MD 21229
Website: www.chinyereudeh.com
Email: allmarthaswriters@yahoo.com

Ordering Information:
Quantity sales. Special discounts are available on quantity purchases by corporations, associations, and others. For details, contact the publisher at the address above.

Library of Congress Control Number: 2020925339

ISBN-13: 978-173636-788-9 [Paperback Edition]
978-173636-780-3 [Hardback Edition]

The prison walls do not change people; people inside the prison walls change each other from bad to worst or from good to best. I choose to be changed from better to best. Behind the walls is a city inside another city. Everything goes—corrupt system, drugs, sex—and money controls the prison facilities. Not all correctional officers are corrupt; but many corrupt officers are always trying to recruit new and good officers to be corrupt like them through making friends with them, dating them, and intimidating them. I was one of the few correctional officers who refused to drop their panties down, be corrupt, or be intimidated by the people inside the system. The story of how I became a female correctional officer II started this way: Growing up as a child in Nigeria, I have always admired the American criminal justice system. Out of the admiration came a burning passion. I spent most of my free time as a kid watching TV shows and movies that involve the FBI, CSI, CIA, Department of Defense, and Department of Homeland Security. Watching all these movies and shows gave me the idea that in America, justice is served to the victims while the offenders are punished to the fullness of the law. As a result, I developed a full-blown interest in becoming part of a system that brings justice and fairness to the unjust.

Also, having a dream to one day aid in making this earth a better place for all humanity motivated me as well. I left my home country at a young age to come to the United States for a better life and opportunity. When I arrived in America, I went back to high school to complete my tenth, eleventh, and twelfth grades at Owings Mills High School. I was placed in the ESOL program so that I could learn the American way of writing and speaking as I came from a British English-speaking country. I came into the United States during the last quarter of my tenth-grade year. Still getting myself familiarized with the new country and school

I came in, I became a C+ student for that year. After mastering and adopting well into my new country, on my eleventh grade, I became an A+ student. And on my twelfth grade, I maintained my academic standing.

Before I graduated from Owings Mills High School, I became an instructor aide in a science and technology class. Furthermore, I received many awards and certificates such as first quarter perfect attendance on November 14, 2008. Along with that are the following awards: a certificate award for excellent behavior and work habits on November 18, 2008; second quarter perfect attendance on February 6, 2009; and an award for outstanding effort on February 19, 2009. I also got another award for academic improvement in the overall ESOL Department on June 8, 2009. An Owings Mills High School Certificate of Excellence was awarded to me for my perfect attendance from 2008 to 2009 in the overall ESOL Department. Additionally, on February 19, 2010, perfect attendance certificate for the second quarter was awarded to me. Finally, a certificate of perfect attendance for the third quarter was also given to me on April 30, 2010. In conclusion, I graduated from Owings Mills High School in May 2010 with a grade point average of 2.65 and ranked 122nd in a class of 239. I outranked approximately 117 students.

After my high school year, I went to Baltimore City Community College to further my education. Just like almost all the immigrants that come to America, nursing is somehow known to be an ideal career, so I was pushed toward majoring in nursing. Family members advised me to take up nursing. Friends encouraged me, and relatives sang it as a song to my ears. I was told that immigrants mostly do not get to the height of their career in America's justice system, especially a female immigrant like myself. I was also informed that it was how the United States system operates. Despite all the discouragement and warnings that were given to me, I still went ahead to follow my passion for building a better society for all humanity and bring justice to the unjust. Against all the advice, I went and applied to become a correctional officer. Being a correctional officer was supposed to serve as a stepping stone to my major career in the mainstream American justice system, but I was wrong.

On December 1, 2014, I was hired as a correctional officer for the Department of Public Safety and Correctional Services (DPSCS) and was posted at the Baltimore City Correctional Center (BCCC) in Downtown Baltimore.

In the middle of December, I left for the training academy of the Police and Correctional Training Commission in Sykesville, Maryland. While in the correctional training academy, I ran into Lieutenant Mary, who for no reason hated me. She did all she could to make sure that I never become a correctional officer. But my self-determination was too strong. Also, my dreams were too real to be killed by her unprofessional manner. Lieutenant Mary focused more on my body type and voice instead of providing me with the necessary tools to become an excellent correctional officer. In the academy, I was everything that Lieutenant Mary wanted to be all her life but could not. My body was formed like an African goddess—thick thighs, big butt, tiny waist, flat belly, big breasts, pretty face. I have dimples on the two sides of my face, pointed nose, pillow voice, and a well-endowed body. I looked like take-away cheesesteak sub. I was morally upright, self-confident, self-assured, had high self-esteem, self-motivated, self-driven, self-empowered, highly educated, and a natural-born leader.

A rule in the correctional academy training states that "any recruiter who has four demerits will be withdrawn from the academy and back to his or her institution." With that being the case, Lieutenant Mary, out of her jealousy toward me, gave me three demerits all at once two weeks before I was to graduate from the correctional academy training, a result of a circumstance that was beyond my control. The event that led her to give me three demerits all at once happened this way: I was involved in an auto accident as I was coming back from the academy training on a Friday two weeks before graduation. As a result of the car accident, I was rushed to the hospital by the EMT on the accident scene. Before I left the academy grounds that Friday, all the recruiters were told to report to a Baltimore location for a shakedown on Monday. We were all told to bring our ID cards. However, I was not able to get out of the hospital until Sunday night, so my brother brought my uniform. Unfortunately, he forgot my correctional officer's ID card at home. So, on Monday, when I got to the shakedown place, I discovered that I didn't have my ID card. Before entering the jail, Lieutenant Mary asked this question: "Is there anyone here who is not with their ID card?" Being the honest human being that I am, I identified myself. Lieutenant Mary took it as an open invitation to yell at me, telling me, "Miss Perfect, do you think you are cute?" I tried to explain to her what I went through and what happened. She responded by saying, "Ain't no one got time to hear your sad story." She sent me back to the Sykesville academy. When I got to Sykesville, I learned that Lieutenant Mary already made a phone call ahead of my arrival. She ordered them to put me to work by shredding all the papers that were in the Sykesville academy ground. I was standing for hours shredding papers and carrying boxes full of papers up and down the stairs. Then it got to the point where I started feeling dizzy, weak, and in pain because I have not had the opportunity to take my medication. I informed the lady in the academy that I needed to take my medication and that I was having pains. She told me that Lieutenant Mary gave her an order for me to continue working until she got back from the shakedown. When Lieutenant Mary returned from the shakedown, she gave me three demerits at once without hearing me out. On that same day, I was told by my fellow recruits that a lot of other recruits that did not have their ID cards with them were allowed to enter the jail by Lieutenant Mary.

I wrote Lieutenant Mary up for denying me the right to take my medication, abuse of power, inflicting cruelty, and unusual punishment under the US Eighth Amendment and also of unfairly giving me three demerits all at once. Lieutenant Mary tried to retaliate by finding means to send me back to the institution and by giving me one more demerit. But she could not because two other high-ranking officers—Sergeant David and Lieutenant Mark—intervened on my behalf. Did I mention that Lieutenant Mark is a tall, handsome, light-skinned black man? He has a muscular, good-looking body and looks sharp in his uniform. He has red lips, white teeth, pointed nose, and brown eyes. He has a nice smile, smells good, and talks right. He is also gentle, kind, and caring. Above all, he is a good leader and an impartial human being—a man who sees human beings as humans, not as a color or race.

Then I dislocated my shoulder while in the academy a week before graduation—a result of another fellow recruit accidentally sitting on top of my shoulder while trying to apply her self-defense training. In the academy, my roommate and I got along well, but some female recruits ganged up on me for no reason.

On January 30, 2015, Friday, I graduated from the academy; and on February 2, 2015, I began my career as a correctional officer I at the BCCC (an all-male prison facility). My assigned field training officer (FTO) was Corporal James on the seven-to-three shift. On March 13, 2015, Friday, I completed the FTO training and was placed on the three-to-eleven shift. Unfortunately, from August 2015 to 2019, I was discriminated, harassed, bullied, dehumanized, received a death threat, and attacked by BCCC ex-inmates. I received underpaid wages, unpaid wages, and reduced pay increase. There was interference in my leave hours and in the time card clocking-in system, and I was issued false medical documentation. Furthermore, the intentional denial of job opportunities, verbal threats, illegal attempts to terminate me from state service, sustained internalized trauma as a result of work-related stress, medically mislabeling of a disability, and unlawful termination altered my future and depreciated my employment market value. These were done by the following people: Corporal Patricia, Corporal Linda, and Corporal Elizabeth. They were all eleven-to-seven-shift female correctional officers. Next are Corporal Maria, Corporal Charlotte, Corporal Dorothy, Corporal Karen, and Corporal Helen (all seven-to-three-shift female officers except Corporal Helen, who is on the three-to-eleven shift). Additionally, there was Captain Donna (seven-to-three shift), Captain Ruth (seven-to-three shift), Captain Michelle (three-to-eleven shift), MRDCC Chief Security Mark, MDRCC Assistant Warden Jeffrey, MDRCC Warden Kimberly. Also included are Doctor Robert (neuropsychologist), Mister Raju of the DPSCS EEO, female officers from the Chesapeake Detention Facility (CDF), Major Angela, female officers from Deputy Commissioner Thomas's office (O'Brien House), Warden Rebecca (CDF), Miss Pamela (DPSCS manager of the Employee Relations Unit), and Doctor Ghansham (DPSCS state medical director).

Meanwhile, I was working on the three-to-eleven shift and got along with all the officers and supervisors on my shift along with all the male correctional officers at the BCCC. On August 2015, five to six months after my FTO training, Officer Patricia started bullying me. She calls me names like, "African Bitch, go back to Africa." Officer Patricia tried writing a false matter of record against me, so I reported her to the eleven-to-seven-shift supervisors: Lieutenant Christine, Lieutenant Richard, Captain Christopher, and Major Brian. But nothing was done about it. After I wrote Officer Patricia up, she went and ganged up with her cliques such as Corporal Linda and Corporal Elizabeth. As I was encountering this bullying and harassment in the workplace, I was also facing issues on unfair wages.

On November 30, 2015, I completed the correctional officer I probation period and was promoted to correctional officer II in December 31, 2015. The state of Maryland standard salary for a correctional officer I started at $38,252 per annum for grade 12, step 3, which is $1,467.44 per week. Unfortunately, I was only paid $1,463.63, which was below the standard wage of an officer I.

Here is the standard wage for a correctional officer I:

CORR OFFICER I

Correctional Officer I
Recruitment #12-004080-002

DEPARTMENT	Department of Public Safety and Correctional Svcs
DATE OPENED	1/10/2014 1:10:00 PM
FILING DEADLINE	4/21/2016 3:15:00 PM
SALARY	$38,258–$54,186/year plus benefits
EMPLOYMENT TYPE	Full-Time
HR ANALYST	Sharon Grant
WORK LOCATION	Allegany Anne Arundel Baltimore City Carroll Charles Howard Queen Anne's Somerset Washington County Wicomico

GRADE

12

LOCATION OF POSITION

Multiple positions are located throughout the State of Maryland.

Main Purpose of Job

Correctional Officer I is the entry level of work involving the custody, security and supervision of adult inmates in a correctional facility.

POSITION DUTIES

The standard salary for a correctional officer II in the state of Maryland for grade 13, step 4 was $1,618.10 per week with a total of $42,186 annually, which came into effect July 6, 2016. However, as a correctional officer II, I was still earning $1,463.43, which was below the state of Maryland's standard salary for a correctional officer I, starting from January 5, 2016, to July 5, 2016, together with a below $50 shift differential and overtime. From July 19, 2016, to August 16, 2016, I was still earning $1,520.98. This is below the state of Maryland's standard salary for a correctional officer II.

Hence, in August 2016, I filed for underpayment of wages grievance. Thereafter, a union member, Frances, filed low-wages grievance on August 26, 2016. Step 2 grievances were made on September 7, 2016; and step 3 grievances were also filed on September 23, 2016, following the September 29, 2016, notice of settlement conference. Then a notice of hearing was filed on December 21, 2016. Finally, a settlement agreement was made by Judge Mary, the administrative law judge, on February 28, 2017.

As the issue of low wages was going on alongside with the harassment, other incidents also occurred such as getting punished for defending inmate kitchen workers, taking one milk and cereal from the BCCC kitchen, and an ex-inmate attacking me in the parking lot. One thing that I have learned throughout my career as a correctional officer II at the DPSCS is that they spend most of their time chasing shadows and worrying about the wrong things that don't make sense. Officers working in the jail get punished for the dumbest things like milk and cereal. Supervisors worry about things that don't matter and disregard essential safety issues. Anyway, the milk-and-cereal matter of record goes like this:

Matter of record: Joyce milk-and-cereal incident

On September 14, 2016, Wednesday, at approximately 2:55 p.m. I, Officer Margaret Rose, went to the kitchen and asked inmate NaG to give me one milk and one cereal. Inmate NaG went to get the milk and the cereal. Shortly after I heard dietary aide Joyce yelling at inmate NaG, asking him what he was doing there. I immediately went inside the kitchen and apologized to the dietary aide Joyce, telling her it was me that sent NaG to get me one milk and one cereal. Joyce was facing the wall using her right hand to tap the top of her hair, saying, "Those are counted." Still facing the wall touching her hair, I asked her, "What does that mean? Does it mean that I cannot get the cereal and milk?" She didn't respond, so I told inmate NaG to hand me one milk and one cereal, which he did. On my way going out, Joyce started yelling at the inmate workers, telling them, "Niggas, I don't want y'all giving these people no shit no more." I told Joyce, "Ma'am, please watch your mouth. These people [inmates] are still human beings like us," and I left. However, I was never reinformed that officers cannot take anything from the kitchen. I always see Joyce giving inmates things like chicken during chicken day, cereals, cookies, and milk. She also gives center hall officers cookies, milk, and cereals. So I thought it was okay for me to go and ask for one milk and cereal.

End of report.

Ridiculously, I got punished by Captain Teresa. I wrote her up but never turned the paper in to the right people because of fear of being retaliated against. At DPSCS, they have a doctorate honors degree in retaliation, compromising their policy of no-retaliation, thinking that we don't know. We all know what time it is. Y'all ain't fooling nobody.

Here is the Captain Teresa write-up:

On September 15, 2016, Thursday, Captain Teresa violated my Eight Amendment right, which is a cruel and unusual punishment. On September 15, 2016, Thursday, at approximately 2:40 p.m., Captain Teresa told me that she would like to talk with me. At about 4:30 p.m., I, Officer Margaret Rose, came out for my lunch break and went straight to the lieutenant's office. I asked Captain Teresa if she still wanted to talk to me, and she stated yes. She told me to come to the lieutenant's office. As I went in, I saw Lieutenant David, Lieutenant Ava, and Captain Teresa. She asked me to sit down, which I did, and afterward, she brought out a matter of record written by CDO Joyce. After I read her matter of record, I noticed that Joyce misspelled my name as she wrote "Margie Rose" while my name is Margaret Rose. I told Captain Teresa that technically, she wasn't directly writing about me on her report because my name is not Margie Rose. Captain Teresa asked me if I want to be technical, to which I answered, "No, ma'am." She asked me what happened between the kitchen worker Joyce and me. I informed Captain Teresa that yesterday, September 14, Wednesday, I asked one of the inmate kitchen workers, inmate NaG, to give me one milk and one cereal. Inmate NaG went to get the milk and the cereal. Then I heard CDO Joyce yelling and questioning what he was doing there. I told the captain that I immediately came inside the kitchen and apologized to CDO Joyce. I notified her that I was the one who sent inmate NaG to get me one milk and one cereal. I also told Captain Teresa that CDO Joyce was facing the wall using her right hand to tap the top of her hair, saying, "Those are counted." I told Captain Teresa that I asked CDO Joyce if I was wrong to ask for cereal and milk because at that time, I wasn't sure if I was wrong in asking for the cereal and milk. So I asked her if I could get what I requested. She did not respond, so I told inmate NaG to hand me one milk and one cereal, which he did. Captain Teresa didn't let me finish the part where CDO Joyce was yelling at the inmate kitchen workers, calling them niggas and stating to the inmate, "I don't want y'all giving these people no shit, no more." She didn't allow me to explain to her why I told CDO Joyce, "Ma'am, please watch your mouth." I said that to her because of the way she was calling the inmates names all because of the one milk and one cereal that I took. Also, I told Captain Teresa how CDO Joyce gives inmates food items like chicken on chicken days and cereals, cookies, and

CHINYERE UDEH

milk to other officers. She also brings to center hall officers cookies, milk, and cereals. I told her that I thought it was okay for me to go and ask for one milk and one cereal to eat. Captain Teresa said, "Margaret Rose, you are smart enough to know when somebody says something has been counted." She also told me, "You are in school, and you do counting for a living." She also told me that she needed a matter of record from me before 5:30 p.m. I told her, "Okay, but I'm still on lunch break. Moreover, it's almost the five o'clock count." She said to me, "You should have eaten before coming to me." She later told me to turn in the matter of record before the end of that day. I told her, "Okay, thanks." As I was about to leave, she asked me if I need a step-by-step help on how to write the matter of record. I told her yes because I have never written a matter of record about one milk and cereal before. Captain Teresa told me to stand up and go back to the housing unit. I told her, "Okay, ma'am, but I'm still on my break. Could I go and eat and then go back to the housing unit?" She told me, "No, go back to your post." I asked her if I could use the bathroom before going back, she said, "No! You should have used the bathroom before coming to see me." I answered her, "Okay, can I please go and pick up my bag from the officers' dining room and drink water?" She told me, "No." I said, "Ma'am, please, I need some food because my sugar level was low." She didn't let me finish, and she still asked me to go back to my housing unit. I obeyed her direct order and went back to my post when I was still supposed to be on my lunch break. As a result of not being able to eat, I started feeling weak and dizzy because my sugar level was low, and the captain didn't give me the chance to tell her that I needed to get some food. I called Lieutenant Ava and informed her that I would like to go home because I was not feeling well. She told the duty sergeant, Sergeant Lucas, and I clocked out and went to Patient First for immediate medical help.

End of Report.

After this milk-and-cereal incident, on May 30, 2017, an ex-inmate attacked me at the BCCC parking lot. The police were called, and the DPSCS Internal Investigation Unit (IIU) was also notified. An investigator came to interview me while I was working at the BCCC, and he promised to return and solve my case, but he never did. So DPSCS closed my attack case as if nothing happened.

On July 6, 2017, Thursday, while working at the BCCC North Wing Lower, I witnessed a female officer named Corporal Maria, who works on the seven-to-three shift, came in for overtime during the three-to-eleven shift. She was flirting with a male inmate, Noah. Going into detail about Corporal Maria's behavior: she opened her leg, brought her hair down, and touched herself. The inmate, on the other hand, was standing between Corporal Maria's legs, holding his private part. Inmate Noah gave Corporal Maria a small white paper when she came back. Inmate Noah stated this to her: "Have you been taking care of that for me?" Corporal Maria responded, "Not yet." Corporal Maria was also blowing kisses at the inmate. In accordance to the DPSCS policy (50), I reported Corporal Maria's unprofessional and unethical conduct to her supervisors, Major Brian and Captain Donna, by writing a matter of record.

On July 19, 2017, Wednesday, while working on South Wing Lower post during my three-to-eleven shift at BCCC, seven-to-three-shift female officers Corporal Maria, Corporal Elizabeth, Corporal Charlotte, and Corporal Ella came to my post with intimidating faces. These officers belong to the same clique together with some supervisors. Both Corporal Maria and Corporal Margaret demanded that I should go back and rewrite the matter of record that I wrote. According to them, what I saw never happened. When I refused, they both verbally threatened me by saying, "We will destroy your reputation in DPSCS and will tell everyone that you are flirting with inmates."

I reported the two officers to their seven-to-three-shift supervisors the next day, but nothing was done about it. The female officers from the eleven-to-three shift ganged up with the seven-to-three-shift female officers and increased their level of bullying, harassment, and the utilization of inmates to hurt me; but they all failed. Because at the end of the day, a dog knows who his or her true owner (master) is, just like the inmates know the difference between a fake correctional officer and real correctional officer. I kept reporting this ongoing hostile work environment to all three shift supervisors at BCCC, but nothing was done about it.

Please know that at DPSCS, correctional officers use the inmates to do their dirty work, like hurting another officer, and inmates use officers to get back at a correctional officer. In addition to this, after Corporal Maria resigned, her clique continued messing with me while at work. On July 27, 2017, Officer Charlotte came to my post at North Wing Lower and started harassing and accusing me of flirting with an inmate. The more I wrote these officers up, the more they ganged up against me. And of course, the supervisors turned a blind eye.

As I was dealing with this hostile work environment, I was also encountering issues with low wages and unpaid hours. On October 10, 2017, I received $991.09 (49 hours). On November 19, 2017, I received again $1,598.88 (79 hours). From 2014 to 2017, I was underpaid for the regular hours, overtime, and shift differential pay.

Another event that happened to me was when Officer Helen came back from the correctional academy and started dating my male coworker/friend Corporal Liam. When Corporal Liam broke it off with Officer Helen, she began to have bad blood toward me. She believed that I took her boyfriend from her, which was not true. Officer Helen joined Corporal Dorothy (Officer Helen's field trainer) and Corporal Karen's group, along with the other two groups, and increased their bullying and harassment. I kept reporting to the supervisors about the officers' behavior toward me every time they come to work overtime on my shift, which was three to eleven. Nothing was done to address this ongoing issue. Because of these three incidents, the other female officers from every other jail I was assigned to saw me as an officer who steals boyfriends from other female correctional officers and as a snitch.

Lieutenant Michael tried his best to help by not allowing these three groups of female officers to come and work overtime on my shift all at once, but Lieutenant Michael's method did not last long because these officers started to complain to their American supervisors and friends, so Lieutenant Michael was outnumbered.

An important information to know is that at the DPSCS, natural-born Americans are treated fairly and are given more opportunities than their immigrant counterparts. Also, inside the jail system, Nigerian correctional officers are the most targeted individuals than any other immigrant correctional officers. It goes without saying that I became a victim of the racial warfare between the Africans and the Americans at the DPSCS.

An unfortunate incident happened to me on December 19, 2017, and this event changed my whole perceptions of the Division of Correction (Corruption) that I was working for. On this very day, my innocence was stolen from me, and the DPSCS system failed me by not protecting me. The DPSCS failed on their mission statement, which states, "The Department of Public Safety and Correctional Services protects the public, its employees, detainees, and offenders under its supervision."

A death threat was made on my life by a fellow correctional officer, Lieutenant Charlotte, and Captain Donna notified me about this death threat note that was written and placed in Major Brian's mailbox in the administrative area. This is an area where BCCC inmates do not have access to and is only used for officers and case managers.

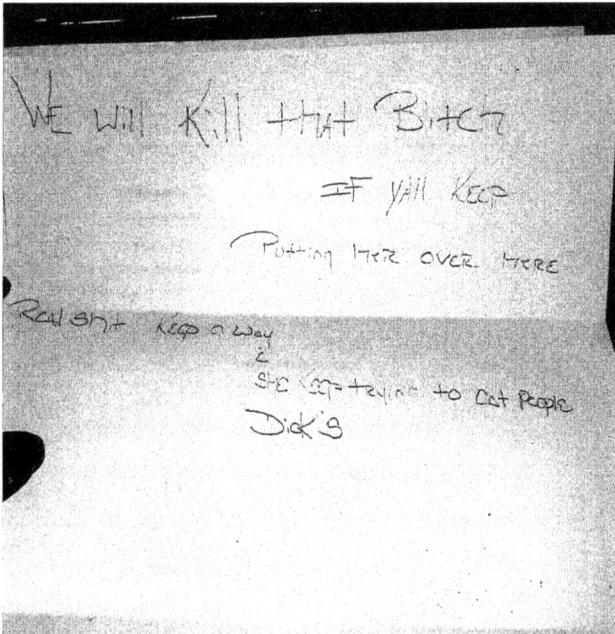

BCCC inmates are locked inside the housing unit, and the only inmate who could enter the administrative area in the front lobby is the sanitation worker who is always escorted by a correctional officer when he cleans the bathroom. Again, I repeat myself, the death threat that was made on my life was from my fellow correctional officers. Yes, by an officer or officers, and they are all females. You all should check this out: 99.9 percent of the attacks that occurs inside the prison system against an officer or inmate are all arranged by another correctional officer or officers or by inmates. This could be due to jealousy, officers hating on the victimized officer, business going bad between inmates and officers, or a love triangle.

In love triangles, there are subtypes: First, a female officer is dating multiple inmates in the same jail at once, and when inmates find out, here comes trouble. The next subtype is when a male or female officer ends a relationship with another officer or an inmate. This relationship breakup is like a *Jerry Springer Show* inside *the big house*. Then there is a male/female officer starts riding on another officer without knowing that his or her girl/guy is equally swinging and giving out the "D"/cookie to inmates like it ain't nothing. Another subtype is when a contraband producer (officer) refuses to supply the demanded goods to the consumers (inmates) or when the consumers refuse to pay the producer the money that was agreed on in order for the producer to meet back with the manufacturer (high-ranking officers/supervisors) for sales and for profit accountability. Similarly, there are another subgroup under the subtypes of prison love triangle relationships: those that involve inmates, visitors/correctional officers' inmates' lovers/visitor on visitor's inmates' relationship drama; officers on officers drawing a battle line for an inmate or coworker; and inmates-on-inmates love warfare. There is never a dull moment in the prison because something is always on the laid-up, off-the-chain TV drama episode and back-to-back unending action that goes on either from the correctional officers, inmates, visitors, case managers, commissary workers, or during inmates' uptown phone conversation. Boy, don't even get me started about the damn phone calls. But going back to the subgroup love affair among inmates' visitors and correctional officers' inmate lovers. This occurs mostly among female officers and inmates' female visitors. This action takes place during visits, when a female officer is working on the visiting post and she happens to see the inmate that she is messing with is being visited by another woman. This visitor could be the inmate's wife, baby mother, girlfriend, mother, or sister. But the female officer doesn't care because she has already concluded that it's the other woman, and here comes trouble between the visitor, the officer, and the inmate. The officer will start giving the female visitor attitude and hard time every time she comes visiting. Oh boy. Inside the housing unit, the officer's behavior toward the inmate will suddenly change, and she will start writing the inmate up for no reasons, but we all know why, and we know what time it is, which is "Shirley is on her feelings." Similarly, inmate's visitor vs. inmate's other visitor relationship drama is another episode for *The Jerry Springer Show*. These issues are mostly encountered by women than men. Two visitors fighting over an inmate who both happen to come visiting on the same day and time. Usually, one of the ladies might be the inmate's wife while the other could be his baby mother, ex-girlfriend, or someone. They always end up fighting each other after the visit. The battle line drawn between officers for an inmate or coworker happens all the time in the jail among male and female officers. Also, there are two types of this kind of war. The first type takes place among female correctional officers, and it goes like this: when two female correctional officers are interested in an inmate, competitions, jealousy, and insecurity creeps in. The funniest part of it all is that one of the officers would, 100 percent of the time, give up her uniform and career to prove her love for the inmate and to win the battle.

It was in the second type of the battle line drawn between an officer and another officer that became a victim. The rules go this way: when a new officer from the academy comes to work in the jail or gets transferred into a new jail, he or she becomes the hottest thing/new meat on the block that every male and female officers, supervisors, and administrators wants to hit on. Moreover, this new officer automatically becomes the new threat and competition without her knowing. This atmosphere of being viewed as a threat and competition among the old officers in the jail results into these three things: officers being overly protective of their properties (male officers), jealousy, and coming up with the means to get rid of the so-called threat, which is the new

officer. In my case, when I came from the correctional academy, I unknowingly became the new fresh meat to eat in the eyes of almost all the male correctional officers, supervisors, administrators, contractors, civilian workers, officers from other jails. I became a threat to the female correctional officers. And as a result, these female officers and their supervisors tried getting rid of me, "the threat." Sadly, but true, anytime the department would send me to another jail, when I get there, I became the new girl on the block and becomes a threat to the older girls.

The last one is inmate vs. inmate love warfare. This situation is bound to happen when two inmates are crushing on one officer, crushing on another inmate, or during a visit when one inmate checks out the girlfriend/wife of another inmate and a fight breaks out between them.

Inside the jail system, I invented the saying, "Check the label before using. If it looks like it's labeled, just know that there is a label on it, leave it alone because it ain't worth it." It goes without saying that both inmates and officers are responsible for almost all the crimes that are committed inside those prison walls, but 101 percent of the time, the institution puts all the blame on inmates.

However, my death threat case was that 1 percent where the inmates didn't play a role or have a hand on it. I will further explain myself. The threat that was made on my life was a result of some female officers' jealousy, insecurity, low self-esteem, and for being viewed as a threat to their correctional officer boyfriends. They see me as a big competition. Throughout my career as a correctional officer, I have never—even for one day—been afraid of the inmates or detainees that were currently serving or about to start serving his or her time. Unfortunately, my biggest nightmare has always been the inmates that put on a mask and wear the same uniform as myself. I am afraid of she-devils, those people who are ready to kill, frame, and destroy my life just because of their insecurity demons; and sadly, they all came in the shape of uniformed female correctional officers. I'm terrified off the daughters of Jezebel that are in the form of uniformed officers, supervisors, and those who are in leadership positions at the DPSCS. People like Miss Pamela, Warden Kimberly, Captain Donna, and Captain Ruth who ganged up and unlawfully terminated me from the Maryland state services. I am not afraid of the inmates because for one, I was trained to withstand the inmates, but I never got trained on how to protect myself around and against the actual inmates who are my fellow uniformed officers. Secondly, I know for a fact that inmates do two things: what you tell them to do and what you allow them to do. Meanwhile, almost all the correctional officers that I have encountered while working at the "Division of Corruption" do more than two things, and the system covers them up. That scares me even more. My attackers have always been officers, supervisors, administrators, and people who are in the DPSCS leadership positions.

It might come as a shock hearing me talk so highly of the inmates rather than the correctional officers and the division in general. I also know that one might undoubtedly begin to wonder if I'm an inmate lover or in a gang because it's unlikely for an average correctional officer to say positive things about the inmates. Well, the truth of the matter is that I'm neither an inmate lover nor affiliated in a gang; however, I am a person who has mastered a high level of understanding of human behaviors, and I see people from their soul level, not by their looks, actions, or environment. Working inside the jail has made me understand that inmates are never the problem. The actual issues that correctional officers face while working in the prisons are the coworkers, supervisors, administrators, and the corrupt system. Inmates are not even on the list. That will go a long way to illustrate some of the main issues that I will be covering shortly. But before that, let me enlighten you all about the lessons that I learned working inside the system: the in-jail education that was taught by the inmates at the BCCC, the positive impact that I created on the inmates, the professional method that I utilized as an officer, the mutual respects between the inmates and me, and most importantly, the healthy boundary that I have set between inmates and me, together with the nonthreatening but not too overly friendly environment.

I know that by now, a reasonable person would start to wonder of the qualifications that I have that would qualify me to talk and write about the issues on public safety and the correctional services. First, I will share a light on my background before returning to the main objective.

Criminal justice is the area I specialized in. I obtained an associate degree in law enforcement and correctional administration at Baltimore City Community College. I have a bachelor's degree in criminal justice and a certificate in forensic investigation at Coppin State University. I graduated with honors degree. I am currently pursuing a master's degree program in homeland security and criminal justice at the American Military University. I will be graduating with a master's degree with honors. Furthermore, I am a member of the West Virginia Lota Chapter of Pi Gamma Mu, an international honor society for the social sciences; the Society for Collegiate Leadership and Achievement; American Military University Chapter of Alpha Phi Sigma Honor Society; Society for Defense and Strategic Studies; American Military University African American Learning Inclusion and Guidance Network (AALIGN) Club; the student government; and a forensic club. I'm also a motivational speaker, former DNA collector, former project manager, and statistics data analyst for the DPSCS in the state of Maryland. Finally, as you all already know, I am a former correctional officer who got terminated unlawfully from the state service.

Now that my background has been adequately established, let us go right ahead with the jail education that I gained from the inmates at the BCCC while working inside the system. Lesson number one, everything one does behind the prison walls affect them when they go back to society. It's easier to turn a *no* into a *yes* than to turn a *yes* into a *no*. Say what you mean and mean what you say. Also, be the same person every day, and don't change the method. In other words, if you are an asshole toward inmates, continue being an ass to the inmates because they will accept you just the way you are. However, they will have issues with the officer who always change on them by trying to be nice one day and then go back into being an asshole the next day. Then again, if you are a supercop correctional officer, which I happen to fall under this classification, inmates will love the officer for that; but there will be trouble in the paradise when a supercop correctional officer tries to become a calm and laid-back officer. Supercop officers are officers that do their job from A to Z without missing anything or making a shortcut. Lastly, inmates go off the chains when a laid-back officer tries to act like a supercop. Laid-back officers are mostly known to be the ones who come to work to get a paycheck. These officers sleep while on the post; they let inmates do whatever they want, and allow inmates in the officers' pod throughout their shift. Most importantly, inmates are highly observant; and they size up the officers, supervisors, and administrators to determine which grade scale to place them in. Mostly, officers are graded based on the way they conduct themselves around their coworkers and inmates, how clean and sharp the officer's uniform is, the officer's grammar, and whether they are down with them or green. The word *down* means you can compromise as long as you will get something in return; on the other hand, the word *green* means you are not familiar with the game, don't know what's up, and are naïve. For the female officers, inmates take note of when an officer is on her period and when she finishes her menstrual cycle. Please don't ask me how, but these guys see and notice almost everything. Funny enough, inmates know which female officers change their hair every month and the ones that get their hair done once in three months.

Moving away from that, working as an officer gave me the opportunity to know the different types of prison gangs and learn some of their tattoo symbols, numbers that are associated with the gang's name, their greetings, formations during mass movement, etc. Their structure during mass movements is as follows: one inmate stands at the back, one in front, another one on the left and one on the right, and their leader is always in the middle of them. In the same manner, most of the gangs that I frequently ran into while working as a correctional officer were Black Guerrilla Family (BGF), Dead Man Incorporated (DMI) Crips, Blood, MS-13, South Side 13, etc. I started knowing about all these things by asking inmates questions as to why they greet some of their fellow inmates with a unique pattern. They unconsciously told me the answer, believing that I was too "green" to understand. Another method that I used to gain information from them was through repeating the words they say to each other during their discussions (I always ear-hustle on the inmates' conversations) and later ask them what those things meant. Any inmate who knew me at that time at BCCC knows that Miss Margaret Rose asks a lot of questions and ear-hustles. Did I mention to you all that I have mastered the inmates' unspoken language of hand signs and mouth opening without them saying anything out loud? For example, some of the inmates' slang words at the BCCC are *Jiffy Mart, Jiffy Lube, grinding, white bitch*, etc. When an inmate talks about Jiffy Lube and Jiffy Mart, they are not referring to the oil change autoshop in Baltimore; instead, they are talking about contraband drugs such as cocaine, ecstasy, flakka, heroin, LSD, marijuana, K2, methamphetamines, mushrooms, salvia, etc. Surprisingly, when an inmate yells on the tier, "Who saw my white bitch?" or "Anyone got a white bitch?" Guys, these precious beings are not talking about a white female. However, they are looking for a lighter to light up whatever they want to smoke. As for me, learning about the inmates' slang words helped me throughout my career as an officer. Also, keep in mind that each jail has their own slang words.

In reality, utilization of professional approach, establishing mutual respect, maintaining healthy boundaries, and creating nonthreatening environment have aided me in understanding the inmates better and in adequately carrying out my duties as an officer. I supervise a total of 128 male inmates by myself on one tier, which totals to 512 inmates; and not only that, I knew each and every one of their names, behavioral patterns, voices, the visitors that visit them, and the cells they sleep in. I can also identify them with their backs turned. Each inmate has about four or more different personalities, and I could tell when something is wrong with them. Throughout my career, I have addressed them by their last names or sometimes I use *sir, mister*, or *gentleman*. I could hardly remember ever calling them inmates or detainees. I treat the inmates fairly, firmly, and impartially while maintaining institutional safety and security. Inmates feel comfortable talking to me about some of their institutional problems such as case management, commissary, visiting, phone (GTL), getting a job, enrolling in church activities, medical, laundry, barbershop, etc.

Back then at the BCCC, inmates were very happy to see me at work and for me to be their housing unit officer. They would always look through the windows while inside the jail and watch the officers' cars as they pulled into the parking lot. Once they saw me, all of them would be yelling, "Miss M, Miss M." The only reason why they were happy to see me was that they know I always come to work with a positive attitude. I equally give them what they are entitled to such as a haircut, and I conduct security rounds. I taught the inmates how to think and act positively. I encouraged them to be the best men for their families. I uplift their spirits when they are down. I taught them about honesty, morals, integrity, forgiveness, acceptance, peace, unity, patience, being virtuous, the importance of dressing, and for them to dress the way they want to be addressed, and, finally, that cleanliness is next to godliness. When inmates are around me, they drop their guard and unmask themselves, revealing their true identities. Sometimes, inmates bring their attorney's letter and case manager's paperwork so I could assist them in reading, and I translate it back to them based on the information that were on the notes. Most times when they can't spell a particular word, they ask me for help, which I do without hesitation. I taught the inmates how to utilize the dictionary and locate words that are hard for them to spell. Inmates always get scared anytime they are about to be released, so they come to me with their concerns and with hope to get some bet peep speech. The most famous bet peep statements I gave to them is, "In the society, cell phones are getting smarter, and the humans are getting dumber, so you all will be just fine. Nothing has changed that much but crazy people." For some reason, after my speech, the inmates that were initially worried would, out of the blue, start laughing.

Treating the inmates like human beings while still doing my job had gained me respect among the inmate population at the BCCC and even outside the jail. For example, there was a time when the cars of correctional officers on all three shifts at BCCC were being broken into almost every day at work. Inmates knew what type of cars that the officers drive without being told. They knew my car as well, but they never ordered their people to go close to it, let alone make a scratch on the car. Inmates on North Wing Upper A side of the tier stated to me, "Miss Margaret Rose, as long as we all are on this housing unit, no one will break into your car." I tried to understand what they are saying, but they left before I could ask them questions. Ironically, my car never got broken into throughout that period. When those officers tried to use the inmates to hurt and set me up, they didn't succeed. Inmates would indirectly say to me, "Miss Margaret Rose, we got your back. People hate on you, people with blue. Be careful."

So the fact that the officers have been harassing and bullying me, together with knowing the location where the death threat note was found, I knew that my threat didn't come from the inmates. I will further explain. After being forced by Captain Donna and Captain Ruth to say that inmates threatened me, I still maintained my word, which was "No, it's the officers." Then I was banned from entering inside the jail, and because of that, the inmates started asking my coworkers about me since they couldn't find me in any of the housing units. When discovered what was going on, the word got to me about inmates asking me "wassup" and if they can assist. I sent the word back and demanded to know who among them placed the threat on me. Word was sent around the jail, among all the 512 inmates, together with their individual gangs. They conducted a four-way check on South Wing Lower, South Wing Upper, North Wing Lower, and North Wing Upper. The result came back negative. Information status was, "We are all straight, no holdup, streets are dried, and no bad blood. Look the other way." Return response was, "Copy that, affirmative."

Captain Donna tried forcing me to sign the death threat package, but I refused. She again tried to force me to say that I do not feel threatened by the death threat note. My answer to her was no. For your information, signing a death threat package is legally waiving off liabilities for the state of Maryland in the event an officer gets killed by either their fellow correctional officers or inmates while working inside the jail. So Captain Donna wanted me to sign my life away together with the right of my family to be able to come after the state of Maryland in the event that I would be killed. Because I refused to sign the paperwork, Captain Donna hated me even more. She reported me to the assistant warden of MRDCC, Warden Jeffrey, on December 20, 2017. After meeting with Assistant Warden Jeffrey on December 20, 2017, Captain Donna ganged up with another supervisor, Captain Ruth. Both women teamed up with the other female officers that have been harassing me in order to increase the level of harassment and bullying. These two supervisors added discrimination, victimization, abuse of power, and dehumanization on top of the abuse that I was going through.

Captain Donna gave an order on December 20, 2017, to all three shift supervisors that they do not allow me to attend the correctional officers' roll call, to eat inside the officers' dining room, and to store my food in the officers' refrigerator. I was eating spoiled food while at work starting from December 20, 2017, to January 12, 2018, as a result of Captain Donna's direct order. On December 20, 2017, I sent an e-mail to Assistant Warden Jeffrey; and then on December 23, 2017, I sent another e-mail to Assistant Warden Jeffrey, updating him about my work conditions and requested for a transfer to the DPSCS headquarters.

The first e-mail that was sent to Mister Jeffrey, the MRDCC assistant warden:

> *Sir, thanks so much for taking time out of your busy schedule to hear me out today. After I left your office, I had the opportunity to open the envelope that your secretary gave me. As I was reading the paper, I discovered that a death threat note was found in Major Brian's mailbox on the nineteenth of this month, which was a Tuesday. I know that Major Brian's mailbox is in the administrative area between the FA's office and the secretary office. Nevertheless, the only people that have access to those areas are case managers and officers. No other person is allowed to go in that area except the front lobby sanitation inmates who wash the two bathrooms but always with an officer who escorts them in and out of the administrative area. It's equally crucial for you to know that the A team is off on Fridays, Saturdays, and Sundays and comes back on Monday. However, the note was recovered on Tuesday, the nineteenth, a day after the A team came back to work. I just thought to let you know.*

The second e-mail that was sent to Mister Jeffrey:

Dear Assistant Warden Jeffrey,

A lot has changed from the last time I saw you in your office about the death threat note that was made to me, which was discovered in Major Brian's mailbox. Sir, after I met with you, my situation at the Baltimore City Correctional Center has gone from bad to worse within a short period of time. Most of the officers on the seven-to-three shift and eleven-to-seven shift believe that I gave you a matter of record, including all their names on it. This false information speculating around the jail has created more negative energy toward me than ever before, which has resulted in me becoming fearful for my life, and that is why I need an immediate transfer to the headquarters before something bad happens to me. Then again, you know that I never gave you a matter of record with officers' names on it, so I don't know where this false news is coming. Mister Jeffrey, the more I talk to you, the more people in my jail hate me for no reason. Reflecting of my last visit to your office, to my understanding, I believed that my post was only going to be in the front lobby until further notice. But I was allegedly told that you permitted them to put me on the outside perimeter wall post as well to keep me from being in contact with inmates. Sir, I was working that post today, and from a reasonable person's perspective, working at the outside post exposes me to a higher risk of being accused or framed up of contraband possession in the state vehicle or, worst-case scenario, even get killed while I'm out there. It's no longer news that most of the people at BCCC hate me and don't want me working there. Please transfer me to the headquarters because until the identities of those individuals who wrote this death threat note and how it got to the major's mailbox is still unknown, I will forever live in fear of being killed inside BCCC or any other jail that

*I might go to as of now. Like I stated earlier, that the more
I talk to you, the more people gang up on me.*

On December 31, 2017, Captain Ruth told me that I was unfit to be a correctional officer. She believed that I was too nice and feminine. Captain Ruth told me that I need to be aggressive toward the inmates. On that same day, she denied me the opportunity of working in the master control center. According to her, my voice is not too Americanized and that I need to sound more like the Americans. Captain Ruth said, "I need you to change the way you talk and sound so that the American correctional officers can hear and understand you." That was another avenue that Captain Ruth used to increase the harassment and discrimination that I was currently undergoing at her hand.

She didn't stop there. Captain Ruth went further by instigating her fellow supervisors from the seven-to-three and eleven-to-seven shifts to harass me more. These supervisors—Sergeant Olivia, Captain Christopher, Captain Donna, and Lieutenant Charlotte—all came one after the other to tell me to change the way I talk and sound and even to change my handwriting. On January 2, 2018, I sent another e-mail to Assistant Warden Jeffrey, informing him about the ongoing victimization. On January 3, 2018, he finally responded. Mister Jeffrey redirected me to the same supervisors that have already been harassing, bullying, and discriminating me.

Third e-mail sent to Mister Jeffrey:

Assistant Warden Jeffrey,

*This e-mail will make it the second e-mail that I have sent
to you, asking that I be transferred to the headquarters
because of my safety concerns. Sir, after seeing the death
threat note that was written for me on December 19, 2017,
and knowing the location where the death threat note was
discovered, which was in Major Brian's mailbox, has left
me with an overwhelming fear. Mister Jeffrey, I'm indeed
fearful for my life. They might kill me just like it was stated
in the threat note. However, sir, I'm not looking forward to*

being killed while under the Division of Corrections' care and for doing my job the right way and being a good officer. Please transfer me to the headquarters before it becomes too late. Furthermore, do you know that as of this moment, I have been restricted from attending the roll call and to eat in the officers' dining room? The worst part of it all is that I haven't been storing my food in the refrigerator. It's equally sad to tell you that most of the time, the food that I bring to work goes bad because I do not have access to the refrigerator. Sir, from where I'm standing, it seems to me that I am being punished for being a good officer that does her job by the book.

From Corporal Margaret Rose

I was still in the process of requesting a transfer to the headquarters when this vital information was made known to me by both the officers and supervisors at the BCCC. They advised me, stating, "Your type doesn't belong to the DPSCS headquarters. DPSCS will rather terminate you first before letting a nobody like you work at headquarters. It's not about what you know but whom you know. You have to suck a dick and bend over before you work at the headquarters. People over headquarters fucked their way into the top/system. That's how DPSCS games go."

When I got tired of being victimized and eating spoilt food per Captain Donna's order, I reached out to the DPSCS headquarters' EEO office on January 12, 2018, at 6776 Reisterstown Road for help. Upon getting there, I was told that the EEO office couldn't help me. A woman from the EEO gave me the DPSCS Internal Investigation Unit number. The lady stated, "If your back was to get pushed to the wall too much that you can't handle, don't come back to the EEO office because we will not be able to help you. Turn to the IIU for help." On January 12, 2018, I called the IIU. The lady who picked up the phone, upon hearing my story, said, "Internal Investigation Unit doesn't investigate a death threat, but we do investigate the death after they occur. The IIU can't help you." Then she hung up the phone.

Shortly after that, I received a phone call from Assistant Warden Jeffrey. He gave me a direct order to report back to MRDCC jail. When

I got to MRDCC, I saw Security Chief Mark and Assistant Warden Jeffrey. Both of them informed me that I had been temporarily deployed (TDY) to MRDCC. Both Assistant Warden Jeffrey and Security Chief Mark tried to convince me into resigning, but I refused. I was told by them that I don't belong in the correction. After Assistant Warden Jeffrey stepped out, the security chief gave me the shocking warning of my life. His statements are as follows: "Officer Margaret Rose, you will get yourself killed if you stay in the correction and try to change the correctional system because the system of DPSCS was meant to be corrupt. You should be in law school. Be a paralegal or minister of God but not a correctional officer. We know that you are telling the truth, but it's easy to say that you are the one causing the trouble than to go and fix the actual problem that we should have fixed before now. The DPSCS will come after your mental ability just like they did to others. Be strong mentally, Officer Margaret Rose."

Female officers at MRDCC started harassing and coming to my face, saying, "So you are that Margaret Rose from BCCC," and many other things. MRDCC and BCCC are only two-minute walking distance, and everybody knows everybody in the department. On January 23, 2018, while at MRDCC, Captain Michelle, friend of Captain Ruth and Captain Donna, started harassing me when I was in 3CM corridor medical unit.

During the time I was working at the MRDCC, I witnessed several inhumane treatment and security issues. However, there is one event that I encountered that stood out. It involves a female officer with a sick son. At MRDCC, correctional officers are being treated like slaves and people that are below human beings. That right there worried and broke my heart. Officers over there were forced to work as slaves. I saw things with my own eyes. Check this out. Ten minutes after I arrived at the jail, I got the clear picture of what was going on. The MRDCC officers, supervisors, and administrators were equally on the Africans-versus-Americans racial war. This time around, it was on a larger scale. The racial war going on at the time that I was there created an impact on the security of the jail—relationships between officers from two different race and nationality—and when it came to responding of the prison code like 10-10, 10-13, etc.

This is what happens inside the MRDCC jail: anytime an American officer calls for a code, all the American officers will respond very fast and on time. Meanwhile, African officers will respond to the same code, but later. Equally, when an African officer calls a code, oh boy, come and see every African run from all parts of the jail, including the ones that are in their post. They would leave their post and start running to respond to the code on time. As you might have already guessed, American officers will take their time before arriving at the scene. That alone was the second thing that I picked up while I was working at MRDCC.

I didn't allow any of the MRDCC supervisors to talk to me in a degrading manner like the way they talk to their officers. There was this lieutenant who happened to be an intel supervisor. She came to me and started talking down to me because I requested to speak with Mister Jeffrey. I immediately shut her down by saying, "Who do you think you are talking to in such manner? I'm a human being, treat me like one." So the lieutenant was surprised that a correctional officer II put her in her place. She later did her homework about who I was then came back and said, "So you are that Margaret Rose from BCCC." I responded to her, "Yes, I am." From that day onward, she started pretending to be nice to me.

One funny thing that happened while I was there: both the American and African correctional officers were confused about my nationality. According to the American officers, they think that I talk and act like them but has a foreign name. Meanwhile, the Africans saw my name as status quo, "One of them." But the only problem they had was that my behavior and the way I speak are more like an American. What happened after was that some of the American officers started saying bad things about the Africans, thinking that I was one of them, like status quo. And Africans will come and say bad things about the Americans to me. Both groups were trying to get me on their side. It goes without saying, I applied some diplomacy just like I did while at BCCC. I started being friends with both the Americans and the Africans. That got them confused even more. Personally, when I look at people, all I see are human beings. I don't see race, color, or nationality. When I was at BCCC, I hung out with both groups on the three-to-eleven shift. A time came when officers at BCCC came to terms that Miss Margaret Rose is not about that kind of life. They always say, "Margaret Rose is not like the rest. She is Americanized and cool." Finally, at MRDCC, the American officers later discovered that I was not who they believed me to be. They stopped talking and being nice to me.

Another thing that happened while I was there was when I encountered a helpless female officer. Her story alone made me shed tears. One day while at my post, a female officer came to me for help. She told me that one of the administrators sent her to me so that I can assist her in writing. She stated, "He told me to come to you because you are the only one who can help me. He also told me that you are good in writing and you are a nice person. Please, can you help me to write a report?" Before she could finish her statement, I told her, yes, I would help her. Meanwhile, as she was telling me who sent her to me, she was crying herself out.

She disclosed the following information: "I work on the three-to-eleven shift. I have a son who is physically disabled and needs more help during the day with his medications and other things. Also, my mother has agreed to watch my sick son at night, when he doesn't require much assistance. Nobody can take care of my sick son during the day or while I am at work. Most times, I leave my sick son all by himself at home to come to work. I call in a lot because we are always in his doctor's office. I have a doctor's note that stated my job should allow me to be with my son during the day."

The officer went further into telling me that as of that time, officers are allowed to change their shift, but when she put in to be moved to the eleven-to-seven shift, she was denied. Meanwhile, other officers are currently being moved from one shift to another.

She continued, "If I knew how to write very well, I would have written back to them, demanding to know why my request was denied yet the other officers were permitted to do so."

Throughout the time she was telling me her story, she was crying. She said to me, "Please help me. I don't want my son to die." With sadness, she informed me that when their previous warden was still at MRDCC, she was allowed to come to work at night and stay home during the day for her son. She further told me that after the new warden and supervisors came in, things changed for her. She mentioned that she needed the correctional job so that her son can continue to have the type of health insurance he has, along with receiving the medical care he needs. After talking about everything, she wanted to know how I was able to move from one jail to another. With kindness in my heart after hearing her story, I asked her to bring all her son's medical documentation to work the next day so that I can make a copy of them. At the same time, I started drafting the first letter of her case, in which the final draft will be sent to the DPSCS headquarters, DPSCS commissioner's office, congressman's office, an attorney, and MRDCC's warden, assistant warden, and security chief. It holds DPSCS accountable in the event anything should happen to her son while she was at work. The administrators and supervisors intentionally denied her the transfer she requested while still accepting and transferring other officers and at the same time undermined the medical doctor's orders. I was going to help her waiver civil and criminal liabilities off herself and put it on the state of Maryland, including having a legal stand to sue the state of Maryland in the event her son dies because of the negligence by the DPSCS. Unfortunately, the officer never came back again after she learned that I was an African. She is an American.

At MRDCC, correctional officers are not valued or seen as human beings. Supervisors and administrators are abusing their power. Not only that, supervisors that happen to be on the lower ranks or are Africans equally face similar issues as correctional officers. Crucial information to know: anytime an officer is found unworthy and undesirable for employment at the DPSCS, supervisors, administrators, other officers, and the headquarters would find a way to terminate the officer using unlawful strategies. I will explain in details later in this book, but for now, this information is what I would like for you to keep in mind: During the ganging up, that victimized officer will be sent to another jail. When he or she arrives at the new jail, false information about the officer has already been spread all over the prison. The same group will merge with the ones from the new jail to restart the harassment. So the officer will start experiencing the same treatment he or she had at the old prison in the new jail. After that, DPSCS headquarters will tag the officer unfit for duty and send the person to the state medical director for evaluation of fitness for duty and for independent psychological evaluation as well. And after that, the officer will be terminated.

Like I said before, I will fully explain later the process by which officers get illegally terminated from the Maryland state service and how some officers get framed up and, most of the time, end up in jail with a label "criminal." Correspondingly, I will expand more on how some of the correctional officers that I had a close working relationship with later became victims of a hostile working environment as their supervisors, administrators, and the headquarters ganged up on them.

Officer Evelyn and Officer William worked with me at the BCCC before they were forcefully transferred to MRDCC on TDY. Officer Evelyn was deemed unworthy to continue working as a correctional officer by Captain Ruth and Captain Donna. The same women who ganged up on me also victimized Officer Evelyn by making up lies against her. Captain Ruth lied that Officer Evelyn physically assaulted her; however, that wasn't true. This was what happened: Officer Evelyn went to Captain Ruth's office, when she was still a timekeeper lieutenant, to find out why her paycheck was incomplete and why the overtime she served wasn't on her paycheck. Captain Ruth got mad at Officer Evelyn and created a lie, which was supported by Captain Donna. This two supervisors were able to convince Major Brian of the lie, and as a result, Officer Evelyn got transferred to MRDCC.

Anytime these supervisors or their group don't want an officer to keep working at BCCC or be a correctional officer any longer, they will create lies against the officer and pass the information to the other group members at headquarters and also in the other jails. When Officer Evelyn got to MRDCC, she started experiencing the same hostile work environment as the supervisors there also harassed her. When I got transferred to MRDCC, I saw what she went through. She told me her story and her plan of resigning as a result of the harassment she was receiving at MRDCC.

I met other officers who were from BCCC and got transferred to MRDCC because both Captain Ruth and Captain Donna made up false stories against them. Officer Evelyn has invested almost fourteen years of her life as a correctional officer and was an excellent, outstanding correctional officer. Sadly, when Officer Evelyn got tired of being abused at work, she resigned. But I stayed on to make a difference. To get away from the bad memories, Officer Evelyn moved out of the state of Maryland, but the move was unsuccessful because she never anticipated losing her source of income from being an officer. Officer Evelyn and I had kept in touch since 2018 when she left DPSCS. When she returned to Maryland, she notified me. Officer Evelyn and I put a lot of effort to get her job back as a correctional officer, but headquarters refused to give her back the job. It's essential to know that Officer Evelyn has a newborn baby, a husband, and two daughters to care for, but she couldn't step up to her responsibilities because of her lack of employment. A DPSCS policy states that an officer who has resigned has up to a year or two to come back to his or her position without reapplying. It goes without saying, Officer Evelyn falls under this provision of former officers that can return to work in less than two years. But she has yet to get her job back.

Another officer is Officer William. This officer is known to be a hardworking person and is an in-service instructor and a self-defense trainer for the DPSCS. He worked together with me at the BCCC. Unfortunately, he got transferred to MRDCC. This was because Officer William was doing his job very well that Captain Donna and Captain Ruth made up a story that he was causing a problem. Officer William gets eight to ten cell phones from the inmates every day. Also, every time he goes in for a shakedown, he comes out from the inmates' cells with a lot of contraband materials found inside the cells. It got to the point that the corrupt officers and supervisors, including Captain Ruth and Captain Donna, ganged up on him and got him transferred so that he wouldn't bring a bad market to them. Right after Officer William was moved to MRDCC, he lost his father. Being the first son of the family, he traveled to Nigeria to bury his father according to the custom and tradition of Nigerian culture. While he was in Nigeria, he was still calling Warden Kimberly's office because the warden gave him a direct order that he should make a call from Nigeria to the United States from Monday to Friday. Warden Kimberly never considered the time difference between the two countries, the phone network service, the stress that comes with losing a father, and having to step up and take the position of a father, alongside the other things that his culture demanded of him in burying his father. He was still calling in like he was told, but something happened in Nigeria that prevented Officer William from returning to America on time. When he came back, Warden Kimberly said to him that he violated some code and that he refused to show up for work. The warden started making up false documentation with the assistance from the headquarters. When the unlawful paperwork was finished, Officer William was forced and intimidated into resigning. Officer William tried getting his job back after he discovered that the documents that he signed were false, but DPSCS refused. Currently, he is still in a legal battle with DPSCS to get his job back after investing thirteen to fourteen years of his life in the state service.

Many other correctional officers are victims as well but are afraid to speak up. What these supervisors at BCCC and the officers and administrators at the MRDCC and DPSCS headquarters do is that they all gang up and illegally terminate officers that are doing their jobs and then turn around and promote corrupt officers.

Another remarkable event happened at the DPSCS that made me realize right then and there that the department was corrupt and lack leaders with integrity. This disheartening incident occurred when Officer Helen came from the correctional academy and started working as a correctional officer at the BCCC. Throughout Officer Helen's seven- to eight-month career as an officer, she made a name for herself as a cop among the inmate population. When an officer gets called by a police inside the jail by inmates, that's an indication that the officer is doing his or her job. Inmates addressed Officer Helen as a cop and me as a supercop. Funny, right? However, things changed. Officer Helen got compromised in the system by the corrupt officers and supervisors of BCCC. To cut the story short, Officer Helen started dating inmates and did not hide her affairs. Every supervisor at BCCC knew about her relationship with inmates, but they turned a blind eye. It got to the point where Officer Helen would go inside the cell of her inmate boyfriend and nobody did a thing about it. As if that wasn't enough, after the inmate that Officer Helen was dating got released from prison, he moved in with her. The funny but sad thing that happened afterward was that Officer Helen took a picture of herself with the inmate while they were together, kissing. She posted it on her social media page with the unknown man's face covered with a Moksha. Officer Helen thought that nobody would recognize the inmate. She made this following comment, "Jesus gave me a brother, best friend, and husband." The picture of Officer Helen and the inmate got to the DPSCS and MRDCC administrators, the supervisors of BCCC, myself, and DPSCS Internal Investigation Unit. After the Moksha was taken off the unknown man, lo and behold, it was the inmate who was released from BCCC. However, the DPSCS IIU, headquarters, administrators, and supervisors covered it up. Officer Helen was still comfortably coming to work at BCCC while I, on the other hand, was placed on administrative leave for being a good officer. The reason they allowed Officer Helen to keep coming to work, according to the IIU, was that they were not sure if the picture they saw was real or photoshopped. Before she resigned, Officer Helen took her time kissing and hugging inmates on the tiers while under the cameras. Somebody had recruited her, maybe another officer or a group of officers. She was part of the group of corrupt officers and supervisors, but she was the only one who left. The others are still there, recruiting more new officers from the academy.

Officer Helen is not the only officer who sleeps with inmates. Almost all female officers at BCCC have or had sexual relationships with work-release inmates. This includes an officer and an inmate who were having sex in the laundry room of the South Wing Upper during the eleven-to-seven shift and another officer was at the door making sure that no other officer came up during the sex. A lot of security-breach events happened—and are still happening—at BCCC that everybody knew or saw but were too afraid to talk about or report. Nine times out of ten, the supervisors they report to are equally corrupt and belonging to the same clique with the officer. Rather than reporting the corrupt officers to the Internal Investigation Unit, Warden Kimberly offers correctional officers who get compromised inside the system a way out by telling them to resign so they are able to receive their state benefits. Also, most of the time, she transfers the corrupt officers to other jails where they go and start forming a new group that recruits innocent new officers like Officer Helen. I know, that's messed up.

DPSCS's policy states that any correctional officer that is seen on the background picture of an ex-inmate will be terminated. Officer Helen wasn't only on the background, she was the one who took the picture while kissing an ex-inmate. But they said, "It could be computer scam." DPSCS IIU forgot that there is something called digital forensics that can be utilized to know the authenticity of an object, image, etc.

On January 31, 2018, at approximately 1:53 p.m., I reached out to the secretary of the state through e-mail for an assistance; but he didn't respond. So when I went to work on the same day at MRDCC, I collapsed as a result of all the dehumanizing and victimization treatment that I received from 2015 to that day. When I woke up, I saw myself in Mercy Hospital.

After I returned to work on February 13, 2018, I was sent back to BCCC per my request. I got along with all my coworkers on the three-to-eleven shift at that jail. There were only a few female correctional officers from seven-to-three and eleven-to-seven shifts that bully and harass me when they work overtime and extend to my shift. I made the request to be sent back to BCCC because officers that were on the three-to-eleven shift were never the problem. The supervisors on my shift weren't a problem either. Instead, my victimization came from officers and supervisors of the two other shifts. Also, I'm more familiar with the BCCC inmates, and I know that the likelihood of them harming me was lesser compared to the other inmates from another jail.

Old things can never change. Female officers Captain Donna and Captain Ruth continued with their victimization of me after I came back to the BCCC. Nevertheless, all my coworkers on the three-to-eleven shift were so happy to see me. We were all hugging each other, and they were saying to me, "We missed you, Margaret Rose. The three-to-eleven shift was so down after you got TDY. There was nobody to make us laugh or lift our spirits." Major Brian hugged me, and he said, "Welcome back home." The whole jail was filled with excitement when I came back to the three-to-eleven shift. There was also excitement when I entered the housing units to greet some of my coworkers who were working there. In each unit I went in, all the inmates were yelling, "Miss Margaret Rose is back! Yes, we miss you!" Inmates in all the four housing units were dancing. Some were jumping, and others were screaming, "Margaret Rose!"

The happiness didn't last long. On February 14, 2018, Captain Ruth came back with her best bullshit. This time around, she told me to write a matter of record that I disobeyed her direct orders. She wanted a matter of record and requested for one. I gave her the write-up she requested.

February 15, 2018

Captain Ruth is after my life.

> *On February 13, 2018, Thursday, at approximately 2:40 p.m., I, Corporal Margaret Rose, was in the front lobby getting processed when I saw Captain Ruth standing in the lobby, watching the officers' shakedown process that was going on. The two officers that were conducting this shakedown were Sergeant E. Olivia and Corporal Amelia. Corporal Amelia was patting the officers down while Sergeant Olivia was at the x-ray scanner checking the officers' bags. When it was my turn, Sergeant Olivia checked my bag, and Corporal Amelia patted me down. I was cleared to enter the jail by both Corporal Amelia, who happened to be the front lobby officer, and Sergeant Olivia, who checked my bag. Meanwhile, Captain Ruth was standing, watching them throughout the process. After that, I went into the bathroom to fix my uniform before going inside the jail.*
>
> *Surprisingly, when I came out from the bathroom and about to pick up my bag that has been checked, Corporal Amelia said this to me while looking at Captain Ruth: "The ChapStick is not allowed." I told Corporal Amelia that I would not bring it again tomorrow. But as I was stepping an inch away from Captain Ruth and Corporal Amelia, Captain Ruth, who was standing and watching me clear the shakedown, stated to me, "You are not going in with the ChapStick. Go back to your car and drop it or trash*

it." Knowing that she has ill feelings toward me and she can go to any length to get back at me for writing her up, I expressed my First Amendment right by asking her why. Captain Ruth also told me to go back and drop my lotion, spray, and ChapStick just to spite me. Please note that both male and female officers at BCCC come to work with the same ChapStick just like mine, but none of them have ever been asked by Captain Ruth to go back and put it in their cars. Also, female officers at BCCC come into the jail with bigger hand lotions and spray than mine. (Check the officers' lockers or stop by during the shakedown of the three shifts and see for yourself.)

Furthermore, it will interest you to know that inmates are having the same ChapStick just like mine and Captain Ruth never asked them to go back to their cells and drop them. Work-release inmates take their ChapStick in and out of jail (check the work release logbook at the front lobby and see for yourself). Sad but true, Captain Ruth's hatred toward me has blinded her sense of judgment and professionalism when it comes to passing fair judgment toward anything that has my name on it. And with the level of detestation she has against me, it will lead her to cause bodily harm or even death on me. After I wrote her up, she has been looking for ways to cause me pain, to stress me out, make me lose my job, and even to kill me as well. Her hatred toward me increased right after December 19, 2017, when a death threat note was written to me and I refused to sign the package, stating that I don't feel threatened. Captain Ruth intentionally took advantage of being the BCCC timekeeper to mess with my paycheck by putting incorrect information on my hours in the system so that my paycheck comes out wrong. Also, anytime I went to her office to ask her questions about my paycheck that always come out incorrect, she yells at me. (Run an account audit on my pay starting from 2015 till the time clock in the system come out.)

Moving forward, on December 31, 2017, twelve days after I refused to sign the death threat note, Captain Ruth started harassing me. She kept picking on every little thing about me; for example, she would tell me, "I need you to change the way you talk and your voice before you work in the master control so that other officers can understand you. And if you can't change it, you can't be a master control officer." She complains about my handwriting and the lemon inside my clear container, and now it's ChapStick, lotion, and spray that everybody else has inside the jail, including inmates. Captain Ruth is abusing her power by looking for fault in everything I do. This is to intimidate me and retaliate against me for writing her up. Her hatred toward me didn't stop at her picking on me for her gain or trying to get me in trouble but went on to the extent of her covering for the officers who wrote the death threat note to me. She tried making me look like the bad officer to hide the truth behind that note. At this point, please know that Captain Ruth can do everything within her power to see me get in trouble, get hurt, and even get killed because of the hatred she has for me. I'm afraid that one day, out of the hatred she has toward me, she will send somebody to kill me. Captain Ruth's hatred toward me has not only created a negative working environment but also impacted my health to the extent that I fainted while working as a TDY officer at MRDCC and was rushed to Mercy Hospital emergency room in an ambulance. (I have medical documentation as proof.)

While I was in the emergency room, the doctor informed me that I was medically okay but fainted because of stress. Also, I went for an annual checkup on January 18, 2018, and the results came out fine (I have a medical record to prove it), and thirteen days later, I fainted while at work. Again, I don't have any medical history of suffering from an illness that can warrant me to faint. Believe it or not, my fainting was as a direct result of Captain Ruth, because both my primary care doctor and the ER doctor found me medically fine. (I have medical record as well.) Captain Ruth's ill feelings and ill behavior toward me has caused a health issue for me that landed me in the ER. At this point, I don't know why Captain Ruth is after my life. Why does she want to see me in pain? Why does Captain Ruth want to see me dead? Why does she want to kill me? Why does Captain Ruth want to make me lose my job? Why does she hate me with so much passion? And why can't she just let me be or see me happy? She has taken a particular interest in me after I refused to sign the paper that will take the liability off the state of Maryland in the event something terrible happens to me.

Please, Warden Kimberly, Assistant Warden Jeffrey, Security Chief Mark, and Major Brian, can you all tell Captain Ruth to leave me alone before she chases me to my early grave? Let it be on record on the above date that Captain Ruth should be held responsible if anything harmful happens to me, such as getting killed, raped, or attacked while working as a correctional officer here in the downtown jail or outside. I have not done anything wrong to deserve this inhumane treatment from her. (Interview three-to-eleven-shift officers, case managers, ERW instructor, and Bible study instructors, about my work ethics.) Captain Ruth and her group want me to leave BCCC because they said that I "see too much and talk too much." As of this moment at BCCC, some female officers are having sex with work-release inmates. (Conduct an investigation and see what you all will find out.) I am not causing any problem here at BCCC. Rather Captain Ruth and her group can't stand seeing me because they know that I will tell on them.

Nonetheless, I recently just came back to BCCC from TDY at MRDCC on February 2, 2018, and in less than two weeks of coming back, Captain Ruth is coming up with something else about me. (Captain Ruth is taking things way too personal, and something is not right with this picture.) From where I am standing, I believe that the most critical thing for Captain Ruth to do is for her to focus on finding out ways to stop contrabands from coming in the institution and discovering those officers that are having sexual relationships with work-release inmates rather than putting all her attention on an innocent officer like me. After Captain Ruth was done picking on me about my hand lotion, ChapStick, and spray that everybody else comes in with, including inmates, I decided to put some of them in a clear plastic bag, went back to my car, and dropped the rest. (Captain Ruth always pick on me anytime Major Brian is not around.) Please, can you all tell her to stop causing me so much pain and endless ER trip while at work? (It is now evident to you all that what I am saying is the truth. My problem is not the inmates, it's the officers. And that the death threat note came from the officers, not the inmates.)

End of report.

Forward to warden, assistant warden, security chief, and Major Brian.

Corporal Margaret Rose

I was sent back to MRDCC not because I did something wrong but because of the supervisors, such as Captain Donna, Captain Ruth, and other female officers from the seven-to-three and eleven-to-seven shifts. When I got to MRDCC, I tried to explain to Warden Kimberly the ongoing victimization that I was involved in. She took the side of the American supervisors and officers who were victimizing me. The warden tried forcing me to resign as an officer, but I refused. I asked her if I can go into case management since I already have a bachelor's degree. Warden Kimberly stated, "You are unfit to be a correctional officer. You are crazy. You will let the wrong inmate out and will get stabbed by an inmate. Finally, you will never be a case manager."

I started crying after hearing everything she said to me. After the warden finished yelling at me, she gave me a direct order to return to 3

Corridor. When I got to the post, I couldn't breathe and was holding the left side of my chest. I passed out again. When I woke up, I found myself back in Mercy Hospital.

On February 20, 2018, when I came back to work at MRDCC, Warden Kimberly, Assistant Warden Jeffrey, and Security Chief Mark called me for conference meeting. During the conference, Warden Kimberly tried to force me to resign. Her words were, "You are mentally unfit to be a correctional officer, and you are causing a problem in every jail you get sent to." She forced me to go on administrative leave with pay on February 20, 2018. The female officers, supervisors, and administrators at MRDCC and BCCC created a cover-up story in order to cover the fact that they all victimized, dehumanized, bullied, and harassed me from 2015 to 2018 and that their actions have impacted my health.

All of them ganged up and started calling me crazy, snitch, and unfit for duty. Warden Kimberly and others didn't just stop there. These officers, supervisors, and administrators made sure that the false news of me being crazy, a snitch, one who takes female officers' boyfriends, and one who is unfit to be a correctional officer was spread all throughout the jail systems in Baltimore downtown area. Warden Kimberly and the other officers created a perfect false picture of me and sold it to the DPSCS headquarters. For their story to look real, Warden Kimberly and her partners in crime, with the help of the DPSCS headquarters, went in the department database system and changed almost all my information. My information that was in DPSCS got compromised: leave hours, accumulated leave hours from 2014 till present, pay increase, etc.

As I was undergoing this hostile work environment, I was also still suffering low hours and wages as well. On February 13, 2018, I received 79.2 hours for $1,603.68. On February 27, 2018, a payment of $1,545.69 was paid to me for total hours of 76.4. While I was on administrative leave, 2 percent cost of living pay increase was given, together with a $750 bonus, to all correctional officers, but that was never given to me. From 2014 to 2018, I was underpaid.

The issue of time card clock-in and time clock plus discrepancies happened from 2016 to 2019. For example, on November 5, 2016, the clock-in system had me at six hours annual leave, but later got crossed out. On December 20, 2016, the DPSCS system crossed me out from eight hours' sick time. On February 28, 2017, the clock-in system had me at three different places on the same day, which is salary reduction recovery eight hours, but I was working on the seven-to-three shift. On February 28, 2017, the same system placed me on negative eight hours' salary reduction recovery. Lastly, on another February 28, 2017, time clock had me on personal leave, but I was on annual leave. On March 1, 2017, I was placed on personal leave but was on annual leave. On March 15, 2017, annual leave elapse eight hours (adjustment form was taken off from the system), alongside with eight hours elapsed sick on July 5, 2017. Furthermore, on October 7, 2017, the clock-in system placed me on four different places, which is impossible. One was seven hours annual leave (alternative leave). Next was on seven hours unpaid time (need to request alternative leave). Next after that is one hour sick elapsed, and the final one is negative seven hours unpaid time off. All of these was where DPSCS placed me on October 7, 2017, according to their time clock; however, the truth of the matter is that I can't be in four places at one time. Then again, on October 8, 2017, the DPSCS clock-in system placed me on three different places. First was eight hours unpaid time off (need to request alternative leave), the second was eight hours annual leave (alternative leave), and the last is negative eight hours unpaid time off.

All these were all lies because ever since I started my career at DPSCS, I have never had unpaid leave or anything related to such. They took all the hours that I worked for to make it seem like I didn't come to work and for their story of me being unfit to appear real. On October 9, 2017, the clock-in system again had me on three different places. First was unpaid time off, negative eight hours. After that was eight hours' annual leave (alternative leave), and the last one was another unpaid time off of eight hours (need to request alternative leave).

DPSCS headquarters, Warden Kimberly, other administrators, and time card supervisor Lieutenant Ruth, who was made captain, changed and took all my leave time. Additionally, on October 10, 2017, I was placed on three different places on the same day. First was unpaid time off of eight hours (need to request alternative leave). Next was another unpaid time off of eight hours, and finally, eight hours' annual leave (alternative leave). On October 11, 2017, time clock had me on three different places, which were eight hours' unpaid time off, eight hours' unpaid time off elapsed, and another eight hours' unpaid time off. Moving forward, on October 12, 2017, DPSCS had me on their time clock system in four different places on the same day. One was five hours' sick, three hours' unpaid time off, three hours' unpaid time off, and another three hours' annual leave. Again, I'm only one person, and I can't be in four places at the same time. On October 13, 2017, DPSCS put me in three places at the same time. First was prescheduled eight hours' holiday, eight hours' unpaid time off, and another eight hours' unpaid time off. I was placed on eight hours annual leave and another unpaid time off of eight hours on October 16, 2017. Equally important, on October 17, 2017, time clock placed me on three places: eight hours' annual leave, eight hours' unpaid time off, and another eight hours' unpaid time off. This is how DPSCS took all my leave time while framing me up to make it look like I did not come to work, but in reality, I was at work. The same issue happened on October 18, 2017; November 7, 2017; November 8, 2017; November 22, 2017; November 27, 2017; November 29, 2017; and December 11, 2017.

Unfortunately, this problem of leave time and time clock plus continued in 2018. From January 6, 2018, to January 11, 2018, DPSCS took me off the time clock system. Also, from January 13, 2018, to January 18, 2018, my whereabouts were never accounted for in the DPSCS clocking system. The same thing occurred on January 22, 2018, to January 29, 2018. They took me off their clock-in system, making it seem like I wasn't at work. On January 30, 2018, I was taken off from the clock-in system, and on February 2, 2018, DPSCS recorded that I was on 1.78 hours' annual leave and on the same day was also in 6.25 hours' sick leave. All these are all lies.

The same problem of DPSCS taking all my hours and framing me up continued on February 3, 2018. The time system had me on eight hours' unpaid leave and another eight hours' personal leave on the same day. I can't be in two places at one time! Similarly, on February 4, 2018, they had me in eight hours' unpaid time off and another eight hours' personal leave. PL/SL on the same day. From February 5, 2018, to February 15, 2018, DPSCS took me off their system and also on February 17, 2018, and February 18, 2018. They placed me on unpaid time off for 3.466 hours and another 4.533 sick hours under the same day (February 19, 2018).

All this illustrates how DPSCS manipulates the system when they ganged up and framed up an officer. I'm a victim of a DPSCS frame-up. On February 20, 2018, Warden Kimberly placed me on paid administrative leave. According to the DPSCS policy, once an officer is on paid administrative leave, he or she is entitled to receive the leave hours that were given for each pay period. But while I was on paid administrative leave, I was losing the hours that I have already accumulated from 2014 to 2018. While on administrative leave on March 10, 2018; March 11, 2018; and March 13, 2018, I was taken off the clock-in system. On March 9, 2018, the system had me on eight hours pre-scheduled holiday and on two hours pre-scheduled holiday on the same day. Meanwhile, I was still on administrative leave. In addition to this, March 19, 2018; March 20, 2018; March 21, 2018; March 22, 2018; April 9, 2018; April 10, 2018; April 14, 2018; April 15, 2018; and April 16, 2018 were all taken out of the system. On April 11, 2018, the clock-in system had me on paid administrative leave for eight hours but adjusted entire pay period per Warden Kimberly. In like manner, May 1, 2018, to May 8, 2018, together with May 12, 2018; May 13, 2018; May 17, 2018; May 21, 2018; May 22, 2018; May 23, 2018; and May 24, 2018 were all taken out of the clock-in system while I was still on administrative leave.

February 28, 2018, the preliminary evaluation initial workability evaluation summary stated the following: "Summary of findings: acute stress reaction. Recommendations to employer/agency: continue current status; full report to follow." Furthermore, the initial full medical report stated the following:

> History of Present Illness: Miss Margaret Rose is a twenty-eight-year-old right-hand-dominant female who works as a correctional officer II for DPSCS. She has been with the agency for over three years, and the last day working of her regular duties was on February

28, 2018, where she was placed on administrative leave. She was sent for a workability evaluation for concerns about her mental health status due to erratic behavior and decrease in job performance. On January 31, 2018, she passed out at work and was taken to the ER due to being harassed at work by colleagues, causing her to be stressed and overwhelmed at work. ER evaluated, treated, and released her to work. On February 2, 2018, she went back to work and was again picked on by coworkers, supervisors. She was verbally harassed because of her ethnicity. On February 15, 2018, due to the workplace harassment, she again began feeling overwhelmed and started having headaches and neck pain and passed out while working inside the jail. She was taken to the ER and was diagnosed as being stressed out and released. She returned to work on February 20, 2018, and was later placed on administrative leave on February 28, 2018.

Nevertheless, the state doctor lied on the date as to when I was forced by the MRDCC former warden to go on administrative leave after her countless efforts to get me to illegally resign from the state service failed. It was on February 20, 2018, that an administrative leave with pay got forced on me, not February 28, 2018. Moving forward with the initial workability evaluation. The state doctor included the following in his medical report:

Mental status examination: on her mental status evaluation today, her appearance was appropriate, her speech was coherent, and her affect was normal, and mood was depressed. Her thought processes were logical. There were no obvious deficits in short-term or long-term memory. There were no signs of auditory or visual hallucinations or delusions. The patient denied any past or current suicidal or homicidal ideation. Impression: acute stress reaction. Summary and recommendations:

workplace harassment, which led to two ER visits due to acute stress reactions. Currently, she has no physical complaints, and she gets sad and anxious when thinking about working at her job. On physical examination, there were no functional deficits noted, and her mental status examination was normal. Due to issues with work harassment leading to multiple stress reactions and the anxiety about going to work, I have concerns about her mental health status and will refer her for a psychiatric evaluation to evaluate her mental health stability.

The state medical doctor at WorkPro, which was located in Rosedale 8665 Pulaski HWY. Rosedale, MD 21237, referred me to an independent psychological workability evaluation (IPE) on March 14, 2018, at approximatelynoon. In like manner, my psychological workability evaluation that was conducted by the Neuroscience Team, Inc. at 22 West Road, Towson, MD 21204, reported the following:

> When Miss Margaret Rose was asked about the discrimination, she experienced while on duty, she explained to the referring physician that on arriving at her FTO officer, she found other female officers to be picking on her. She details this as stating to her that she acts too "bougie" (she explains, 'like white folks—arrogant and bossy') and that she speaks too softy. She also says they called her an African bitch. On telling other African coworkers, she was told to 'just manage it, because they pick on all of us, and there's nothing you can do about it.' The teasing grew worse, with her coworkers forming a clique against her, and she reported the behaviors to the officers. Hostile mannerisms and telling her to 'Go back to Africa.' Miss Margaret Rose presented with a log of events. The staff has labeled her 'crazy' or 'bad,' and she cannot anticipate them accepting or working cooperatively with her. Behavioral observations: Miss Margaret Rose arrived on time for

her appointment with us. Attire was appropriate, hygiene well maintained, and she responded with appropriate affect and eye contact to verbalizations. Responses were relevant and focused; there was no evidence of tangential reference. Rapport was easily established, and Miss Margaret Rose communicated with adequate vocabulary and sentence structure. In the testing situation, she applied herself with interest and attention and cooperated with the requirements of the evaluations; as such the results are assumed to validly reflect her abilities. Miss Margaret Rose was tested throughout four hours, during which she applied herself without excessive tiring or loss of focus. There was no indication of psychotic thought process, delusional or hallucinatory thinking. In language tasks, no instances of paraphasia or agnosia were noted. There were no notable signs of perseverative or compulsive thinking or behavior. There were no notable signs of depressive, anxious, hypomanic or manic behaviors. Beck's depression and anxiety inventories, Revision 2 (BDI-II, BAI): Miss Margaret Rose attained scores of 0, which suggests that she is not currently suffering from symptoms of depression or anxiety as might justify diagnosis of a depressive disorder. Bipolar Screening Inventory (BSI): Miss Margaret Rose endorsed 0 symptoms indicative of past episodes of manic/hypomanic phase, and 0 symptoms as current. This is consistent with her personal history which does not include a bipolar disorder diagnosis.

Finally, the doctor, after finding out that I was not crazy after the 2018 psychological evaluation that DPSCS sent me to for evaluation after accusing me of being crazy, he then created a medical report based on a culturally biased IQ exam. His IQ exam stated the following:

General intellectual ability: Miss Margaret Rose general cognitive ability is within the borderline range of intellectual functioning, as measured by the FSIQ. Her overall thinking and reasoning abilities exceed those of approximately 3 percent of individuals her age (FSIO=72; 95% confidence interval = 68–77). These results are surprising, given her academic achievements and general presentation, which seems stronger intellectually than the results would indicate. Perceptual reasoning, Borderline range, above those of approximately 4 percent of her peers. Personality Assessment Inventory (PAI), placed her on a fifth-grade level, where the PAL requires sixth-grade comprehension levels. Regardless of the cause, however, the test results can only be assumed to be invalid therefore no clinical interpretation is provided. Summary: achievement testing found Miss Margaret Rose to be at an elementary school level in mathematics, word reading, and spelling and at a junior high school level in sentence comprehension. The scores she obtained are commensurate with her full-scale IQ, but not career or education accomplishments. At odds with this impression of the patient is her conversational level and demeanor, which seem typical of a higher level of intellect than what was captured in this testing session. In either case, her inability to comprehend communication is likely an impediment to competent performance in work settings. It is also possible that Miss Margaret Rose contributes to her own social isolation through a style of communicating that is interpreted by others as supercilious and self-righteous, without realizing that she is causing this. Though we must acknowledge high likelihood that racial discrimination (even black on black) and disregard of important safety regulations are probably present and observable in the prison system of Baltimore, which unfortunately has history of such. And that Miss Margaret Rose's rendition of her experiences is possible. Diagnosis: borderline intellectual functioning, intellectual disabilities (assumed to be due to cultural background). Recommendations: in the interim, if conditions are as bad in relationships as described by Miss Margaret Rose, she should not be working at the site of her former placement since this clearly would not be safe practice. It appears that she would not receive the support needed to secure a stable situation. In the event she can be accommodated with a change of prison site, she could continue her work in a different locale, and her potential to succeed in this work will be judged by that process. She would do well, however, to engage in counseling and self-educating in culture and custom of the United States, to deal with the work experience and develop in her interpersonal style.

So, after the psychologist reported his false findings and DPSCS forced me to believe that I was disabled and tried firing me from state service, I countered the findings by questioning the credibility of the IQ exam aspect of the psychologist's report. Some of the questions that I asked the department were as follows: If I was reasoning like a fifth grader, with elementary school level in mathematics, word reading, spelling and at junior high school level in sentence comprehension, how come I was able to pass and get this job that was meant for high school graduates and GED holders? How did I manage to go through the academic part and pass the written exams, which was made for college students, alongside the physical exams? Then again, how was I able to perform my duties for over three years before the accusation of having a reasoning like a fifth grader's by the state psychological doctor? I also questioned other aspects of the medical result.

On April 18, 2018, a follow-up workability evaluation was made. The preliminary evaluation summary stated:

Recommendations to employer/agency: okay to return to regular job duties if agency can accommodate her to a new location full report to follow. Doctor Robert noted that she had issues with social skills and management in her current work environment. It was also noted that her work environment did not provide her the optimal social support due to some of the negative social interactions noted by her; it would not be a safe environment for her. It is recommended to assign her to a different prison site.

So, after this first workability evaluation in 2018, DPSCS medically mislabeled me as having issues with interpreting and responding to social situations appropriately, having borderline intellectual functioning, intellectual disabilities, low IQ, and reasoning like a fifth grader's. DPSCS indicated that I contributed to my own social isolation through a style of communicating that was interpreted by others as supercilious and self-righteous and intentionally included a racial comment for me to engage in counseling and self-educating in the culture and custom of the United States. Unfortunately for the DPSCS and their fake doctor, they never knew that America was the home I grew up in knowing and that I'm as Americanized as the American people. The only difference between me and the natural-born Americans is my name. And as for self-educating into the culture and customs of the United States, I had already done that way before I came to America as a young child. Furthermore, on April 19, 2018, DPSCS employee health relation ordered me to write a letter for reasonable accommodation, which I did.

On April 23, 2018, I passed the case management specialist trainee exam and was placed on the better-qualified category. But I was never given the opportunity to participate in the interview after allowing more than four hundred applicants to undergo the case manager's job interview. This opportunity was intentionally denied to me because MRDCC Warden Kimberly stated that I will never be a case manager. This is because she believes that I am crazy. The wardens in each jail play a significant role in determining which officer gets promoted.

On April 24, 2018, the full medical result of the neuropsychological report came out. The result indicated that I was not crazy—which I was accused of by Warden Kimberly, the BCCC officers and supervisors, the DPSCS headquarters, and other officers from the MRDCC jail. Doctor Robert stated in his report that I have low IQ and that I reason like a fifth grader with the comprehension skills of a junior high school student. He also mentioned that I am responsible for my problems because of my fifth-grade reasoning and that I have a problem with English comprehension. In his final report, he included that I need to self-educate myself into the American culture because I am not Americanized. The neuropsychological doctor medically mislabeled me with low IQ and lacking of social skills. I countered the IQ aspect of the Doctor Robert's report because I know that I don't have a low IQ. Doctor Robert used a culturally biased IQ exam that lacks reliability and accuracy to generate his medical findings, thinking that I wouldn't find out what he did.

On May 30, 2018, DPSCS EEO Raju tried to force me to believe that I have a disability that was based on a biased IQ test. I refused to accept the medical label of being disabled. DPSCS EEO Raju gave me a paperwork that said that I have a disability after he and one other woman made an effort to convince me, but they were unsuccessful. DPSCS headquarters also decided to terminate me based on the IQ exam, but I reached out for help from a woman named Mildred at the office of the Secretary of the State. On the same day, May 30, 2018, Mister Raju sent me an e-mail forcing me to believe that I have a disability—which, again, I don't have. On May 31, 2018, I responded to Mister Raju's e-mail, reinforcing to him that I never had a disability in the past nor in the present.

Date: Thursday, Mary 31, 2018, 07:48:42 AM, PDT

Good morning, Mister Raju, sorry that I wasn't able to respond to your e-mail yesterday; however, I wrote the letter of a reasonable accommodation based on the instruction that I was given by the headquarters upon receiving the preliminary evaluation summary, which was on April 18, 2018. The state medical director stated, "Summary of findings: Acute stress reaction, recommendations to employer/ agency: okay to return to regular job duties if a job can accommodate her to a new location full report to follow." These were the state medical director's instructions, and as a result of his summary, I requested a reasonable accommodation. Nevertheless, I received my full medical evaluation report on April 24, 2018 at approximately 2:53 p.m. When I saw the medical result, and after going through it, I saw that both the state doctor and the neuropsychologist stated that I was not crazy. Because Warden Kimberly, Assistant Warden Jeffrey, Captain Donna, Captain Ruth, and some female officers on the seven-to-three and eleven-to-seven shifts made up lies by saying that I was crazy just so I would lose my job. And also to cover up the discrimination, dehumanization, bullying, harassment, etc., that they did to me since 2015 and are still doing until the present. Then again, sir, I saw in my psychological evaluation that the doctor that the state sent me for evaluation lied on the IQ exam aspect of his report. Mister Raju, by law, an IQ examination is not the right method to use when trying to measure people's intelligence because the test itself lacks reliability and accuracy because of such factors as genetics, culture, environment, nutrition, etc. I'm a victim of the impact of this test. Please do your research and see things for yourself. I don't understand why the psychologist that you all sent me to go and see is using an IQ test that has been removed by the Psychological Board Association to pass judgment on me, knowing that his analysis was culturally biased. Why did the doctor that I was sent to lie on his medical report to destroy my future here in America? Sir, why would a doctor make up a fake medical report based on an IQ exam? Mister Raju, haven't I suffered enough at the DPSCS? For over three years, I have been discriminated, harassed, picked on, bullied, intimidated, lied to, had two emergency trips to the hospital while at work, been deprived of the fundamental human rights and needs, eaten spoiled food, and been called crazy. I was also attacked and forced into administrative leave, and presently, I'm facing a death threat. The list goes on and on. Now it's a fake IQ medical report. Tomorrow, it might be another thing. Why is all this happening to me? Why me, Mister Raju?

Why, sir? In all honesty, the reasonable accommodation that was given to me is not reasonable at all because that wasn't what I was told, but I guess a Nigerian life doesn't matter.

Enjoy the rest of your day, sir.

Without it coming as a surprise, DPSCS undermined my safety by placing me in another jail environment and claimed that I requested to be transferred to another prison facility. In reality, the reasonable accommodation that I asked for was to be placed in another position whose requirements I am qualified for based on my degrees. DPSCS intentionally removed me from minimum, prerelease, and work-release jail and placed me with maximum security federal detainees that are still waiting to be sentenced: Chesapeake Detention Facility (CDF).

I know that by now, a reasonable person might start asking how it was possible for me to withstand and defeat the entire Department of Correction from 2015 to August 15, 2019, without a lawyer and to also identify a false medical report that was generated from a culturally biased IQ exam. In general, I will explain in details how I defeated DPSCS, the reason why I'm always three thousand miles ahead of them, and how I was able to beat the system that has been in place before I was born. Also, I will explain what happened behind the scenes that ordinary people don't notice and the methods DPSCS used to get rid of correctional officers.

The DPSCS has formed the habit to bully, discriminate, dehumanize, and wage war on innocent correctional officers, especially immigrant officers. These people go around looking for trouble and punishing innocent officers. Once they get involved with a situation that is beyond them, such as my case, they would all run to the so-called leaders of the department for protection. Knowing that it's the leaders' responsibility to protect the image of DPSCS at all cost, they would try to get rid of the problem rather than try to find out why the issue existed in the first place. The DPSCS leaders always based their judgment on the headquarters' complaint about an officer. The leaders of DPSCS never tried to hear the other side. So, before you know what is happening, the victim will be further victimized. This epidemic is an ongoing issue in the department from one decade to another. There is nonstop corruption, discrimination, intimidation, victimization, dehumanization, etc. The same problems are still currently in place. Almost every correctional officer at the DPSCS has been deeply hurt and scarred by the division where they have been working at. Many can't fight back or speak about the ill manner that goes on inside the department because all the officers has been brainwashed that the system is meant to be corrupt and they can't fight the government. First of all, let me recreate that wrong impression. We are the government. I'm the government, and my voice matters. Not only that, the government is known to be for the people, by the people, and are the people. So, in my dictionary, there is no such thing like "fighting the government" because I'm the government.

DPSCS has made officers believe that they are above the law of the United States of America and that they can do anything they like to human beings and nobody will question them. Every correctional officer who has worked or are still working under DPSCS have been subjected to modern-day slavery and are afraid that people in the system will come after them if they don't play along. From my personal experience, there is a step-by-step method that DPSCS uses to terminate or frame up correctional officers.

After my explanation, one would begin to wonder whether the correctional officers that have been terminated or currently facing criminal charges are really guilty of their crime and whether the ones who are serving their time in a prison facility could have really committed the crimes they were accused of and are being punished for. Could it be a frame-up from the department in general? Most times the first step would start among the officers. This occurs mostly between female officers than their male counterparts. However, in some case, it could be initiated in other various ways, such as a male supervisor asking a female/male subordinate for a sexual relationship and making sexual advances. If the subordinate declined their request, it could result to a frame-up or a termination. Then again, the issue could start from officer to another officer, administrators to officers, supervisor to supervisor, supervisor to the administrators. It could be an issue on racial discrimination, discrimination based on national origin, being a targeted officer, etc. But let me stick to my personal experience.

But before that, it will be a delightful honor to expose some of these false declarations to you all. The department claimed to have a zero-tolerance policy toward discrimination, sexual harassment, and abuse. Yes, on paper they do, but in reality, those stuff don't exist. It's all about trying to make themselves look good publicly.

Now that the first phase of how correctional officers working in the DPSCS illegally gets terminated and framed up have been made, the next step in the process is that the officer would start to encounter some bullying, harassment, and discriminatory treatment. He or she would become a topic of discussions inside the jail and among the inmates as well. The main purpose of this ganging up is for the officer to get frustrated and resign. In some cases, the officer could still manage the situation. Normally, the next stage of victimization is the ganging up, the write-up from supervisors, intentionally denying of any entitlements such as vacation leave hours, personal leaves, etc. After that comes intentional interference of wages, accumulative leave hours, and frequently being placed on a more dangerous post than usual. The next stage is when officers use inmates to try hurting the officer or the inmates, officers and supervisors makes up lies. After that, everyone would be ganging up against the officer and creating false information and presenting them to the administrators. In most times, some officers usually get frustrated, drained, and become tired of fighting. These officers give up in the middle of the fight and end up resigning. Only a few of the other officers make it to the next stage, which is being framed up by the department or seriously get injured by an inmate or gets killed in the community, because at this point, almost everyone in the department has gotten false information about the officer and they are ready to come after him or her. This is the most crucial stage for any officer who is undergoing victimization from DPSCS. Majority of the time, correctional officers get victimized through frame-up or being hurt by an inmate or inmates.

In my case, when I got to this point, I started to experience spiritual attacks together with the physical attacks that I was undergoing. However, immediately after I got to this point with DPSCS, my spiritual abilities went off the roof. I could see everything, hear everything, feel everything. I was three thousand miles ahead of DPSCS in their own game. At this point of the battle with DPSCS, I will highly advise any officer to do four things: one, resign; two, fight to the finishing line; three, put your hope in God and pray nonstop because spiritual attacks are included during this stage; four, go and get stronger voodoos that are stronger than theirs. But praying is the key. Nevertheless, whatever the officer does, please don't give in or give up. Honestly, resigning wouldn't be a good option for any correctional officer because he or she might not be able to get another job. In my case, I applied for almost three hundred jobs, but I couldn't get not even get an interview, let alone a job. It was then I knew that my information had been compromised. I started calling and asking DPSCS what they did with my information because I'm not able to get another job both in and outside the Maryland state agencies. In a sense, I believed that I was blackballed from getting employment.

Occasionally, depending on the officer and his or her aggression in fighting against the ongoing victimization, the DPSCS skips the framing-up aspect and goes directly into creating a false medical report against the officer, just so they would lose their job. State medical directors are the people who provide fake medical reports that have gotten millions of correctional officers illegally terminated from state service. Alongside are the medical reports from DPSCS's independent psychological evaluation. DPSCS often lie their ass off by saying, "We don't control what the doctors write on the medical report, and the doctors are independent body separate from the department." Lie, lie, lie. They are all the same. If all these people are not working together, how come officers have been forced to undergo their medical evaluation through the state doctor? Why couldn't the officers be evaluated from their primary care doctors? DPSCS state medical directors, doctors, and psychologist are paid to create a false medical results for an officer. They are not real doctors in that they are not saving lives.

I will give you an example of how DPSCS's framing-up of correctional officers of criminal activities has impacted the victimized officers such as myself, who is currently suffering from long-term internalized trauma of depression and work-related stress disorder that is yet to be treated. This incident happened in Central Booking, one of the downtown Baltimore jail. A Nigerian male correctional officer was framed up for raping a male detainee while working inside the jail as he was conducting security rounds. I was part of the few officers who were opportune to get close to this case because I was among the officers that participated during his hearing board. After the officer was accused by the detainee, with the support of the officers, Prison Rape Elimination Act (PREA) was called in for investigation. During the investigation, security cameras were viewed, and there was no indication of the male officer and detainee engaging in inappropriate manner or even the detainee performing oral sex on the officer. The camera only showed the officer going inside the inmate cell to make sure he was still alive while he was conducting security rounds. The camera also showed that the male officer went inside the bathroom to check and make sure no detainee got stabbed inside the bathroom, which is according to the DPSCS policy. Notably, a forensic expert conducted an investigation for fluid and body contact of the detainee and the male correctional officer. Evidence showed that there was no body fluid found in the officer, nor was there any contact made. So this officer was innocent of the crime he was accused of, correct? The next thing that happened to this innocent man will break your heart. People from the department released false information to the news channels and included the officer's picture. An innocent man was publicly humiliated when his picture was shown on all the news channels as a Nigerian male officer who had a sexual relationship with a male detainee at Central Booking Detention Center. The man's mother saw a picture of her son on American TV while she was in Nigeria. The case didn't just end there. Someone reported this innocent man to the immigration department. Immigration law enforcement officers came and arrested this man and placed him in immigration detention for reevaluation of his immigration status and possible deportation. This innocent man that got framed up by the DPSCS was a known public figure in the Nigerian community. His late father was one of the most respected, popular Nigerian musicians. Through the unity of almost all the Nigerian Igbo tribe in Baltimore, God's grace upon him, the respect his late father commands in the Nigerian community, and the love the Nigerians had for him as a result of him keeping up with his late father's legacy alive, the Nigerians raised money and got him one of the best criminal lawyers. The man was acquitted despite the false documentation that the department came up with to destroy this man's life. Finally, he became a free man, but his reputation has been damaged for life. Without knowing what to do, he sued the state for defamation of character and won his case.

In my case, DPSCS placed my pictures in all the Downtown Baltimore jails' entry and exit posts. They accused me of being mentally unstable and a threat to all the officers and society. DPSCS made me look like a terrorist. But I was an innocent, harmless person with a good heart who couldn't hurt a fly. After my experience and knowledge of the other cases like mine, I couldn't help but wonder how many correctional officers that are currently serving time are innocent of a crime they did not commit. Equally, how many of them are still waiting for a trial? How many officers have been illegally terminated based on false medical documentation? And how many of these people are still wandering around the community believing that they are mentally sick but in reality there is nothing wrong with them as they are only victims of made-up lies that state doctors made as per DPSCS's request? Almost all the officers in the DPSCS have been scarred for life. The general statement made by all the correctional officers at the DPSCS goes like this: "The system doesn't give a fuck about me, and I don't give a fuck about them either. Am just here to get my check, they need a body. They got a body shit." Another saying goes like this: "We are nothing to them other than numbers, paychecks, statistics, and bodies. They don't care about us."

I have seen where these officers' frustrations are coming from. As a result of their frustrations toward the corrupt individuals who are operating the department, together with the level of corruption that is happening inside the system, almost all the correctional officers would choose, in return, to victimize other people and break the rules after they themselves were failed and victimized by the same system in their workplace. Correctional officers, not knowing the best way to address their victimizations, would decide to victimize other officers. This is the way the game goes. These officers would turn around and victimize the next person behind them. This ongoing victimization at DPSCS began at the headquarters and got passed down through the chain of command until it affected me.

In my opinion, if I was in a leadership position, I would personally release the correctional officers that are currently or in the process of serving a prison term because these individuals are innocent of the crime they are being accused of. Also, these people are the direct products of the DPSCS's corrupt system. These people are victims of a corrupt system. A pot cannot call a kettle black. Meanwhile, if any punishment was to be given, let it start from the headquarters before it goes down to the officers. Direct or indirect, agree or disagree, the truth remains that the corrupt correctional officers are the product of the corrupt system that they were all subjected to. Change the people that are corrupting the system and the officers will change. Corrupt officers, again, are the reflection of the failed DPSCS system. Correctional officers who are working under the DPSCS can never act like reverend fathers or sisters. The prison environment will never be like missionary or a sisters' convent school. Then again, if wishes were horses, I would wish that the policymakers revoke the immunity that has been given to DPSCS that includes excluding them from being investigated by external investigators and allow external investigators such as FBI, CIA, etc., access into the Department of Correction. The DPSCS Internal Investigation Unit's jobs are to investigate unlawful conducts of DPSCS workers, prevent crime, protect, deter, and safeguard the lives of the individuals working in the system. But in reality, DPSCS IIU's significant concerns are protecting the image of the department that is hurting officers, intimidating innocent correctional officers who don't know their rights, and overlooking illegal activities that occur inside the department. From my encounter with DPSCS IIU, all the correctional officers under the DPSCS are members of the union, but in most cases, the union takes the side of the department rather than fighting for the officer. Again, this is based on personal experience. If only wishes could be a horse, I will wish that lawmakers, leaders, public figures, and citizens of this great country America would step in and stop the injustice that has been going on at the DPSCS.

Never in the history of DPSCS has an officer stood up against them and beat the department at their own game. No officer has publicly called DPSCS for who they are—a corrupt system that takes the lives of officers and destroys it. I was that correctional officer who stood up against the corrupt system of the DPSCS. The whole department came at me to ruin my life, but they don't know that he that is in me is greater than he that is in them. And as a result of that, I shall fear no one. DPSCS has done wrong to almost all the officers. The department came at me thinking that I was one of those officers that are afraid to speak. DPSCS drew a war against me, hoping that I will get scared or be intimidated just like the other correctional officers. Unfortunately for them, they messed up with the wrong person. DPSCS didn't know that the person they are fighting against is highly gifted spiritually. In the whole department, only four people knew that I was spiritually gifted. These individuals are the two chaplains, the MRDCC security chief, and the lieutenant at CDF. I'm one of those people that God sent to this earth to aid humanity. I came to this world with my third eye already opened. I see beyond normal sight when looking at human beings. I look inside their soul and discover who they are genuinely inside as opposed to what they might be showing to the world. I came to this earth, but even until today, I still feel that this planet is not my home, like I am only a visitor here on earth. And because of this feeling, I am not attached to anything material or even fame, social status, power, social acceptance, etc. However, the only thing that I'm connected to on this earth are human beings. Everything about humanity bothers me so much. When humans are sad, I am sad. When they are happy, I am delighted. I dislike injustice, unfair treatment, intimidation, corruption, etc. My perception of life is different from an average person. The way I react to things is equally not the same, and things that worked for an ordinary human being doesn't work for me at all. And right there was where DPSCS made the biggest mistake of its life.

DPSCS used the same approach on me that it has been using on other officers, thinking that their plans will work. Some of the spiritual gifts that I was born with include, but are not limited, to the following: the ability to feel other people's pains as if they are mine, mind reading, picking up nonverbal languages, the tone of a writer from their writing, high intuition, and high sensitivity to everything. I also have the ability to see, stop, and predict the future and downloading the information in my brain as well as seeing and living through an incident before it occurs. I continuously stare at the moon and stars, wondering where home could be. Sometimes, I miss the Blessed Virgin Mary. Furthermore, I see right through people, picking up energy from the environment and people, and I have the ability to see and feel danger coming my way as well as the ability to put things in a pattern. Additionally, I can receive messages through a dream. I receive heavenly visitors while asleep, receiving guidance, instructions, warnings, and favors. My thoughts are more powerful than my words, but then again, my dominant thoughts create my reality, being physically removed from oncoming danger or the like.

Now that you all are aware of some of the gifts that I was born with, I would describe more on what my life was growing up with all these gifts. DPSCS had no clue that I have reincarnated two times. The first time was as a doctor and second time was a lawyer, and all my memories and education come in handy when I needed them, as when they tried to play me with a false medical report, their policy, and laws. But I guess now they know.

For a start, my grandmother thought that her grandchild was born as a superhuman, out-of-space kid. At some point, she began to wonder who I was, where I came from, and if there was a mistake in the hospital and she was given the wrong baby. Crazy, right? The reason why she started thinking like that was because I knew a lot of information that happened before I was born without hearing the story from anybody. Also, my behavior and actions were different from kids my age. I talk more like an adult than a child, and I never did what everybody else was doing. In my community, while growing up, you would never catch me being around kids my age. I was more likely to be among adults. I had more adult friends than kids because I was more drawn to bright light and to people who wore white. The people that I was always in company of were reverend fathers, soon-to-be-ordained priests, and reverend sisters. Ironically, I don't like going to church, but I am more than likely to be seen in the Blessed Sacrament chapel than playing with the other kids.

As a kid I enjoyed babysitting and caring for babies. Children and infants love being around me. Nothing else matters to me than to see people happy. On the other hand, I get sad when I see people being hurt or mistreated. I often have a strong feeling that it's part of my duty to make this world a better place for all humanity. Because of that, at the age of three, I joined the great sisterhood of Girl Guides and became a little Brownie. At the age of three, I made a promise to do my best, to do my duty to God, and my country, to help others in needs, and to obey the Girls Guide Law. These were the promises that I made, and until today, I'm still keeping my promises. Wanting to help and serve humanity came normally to me. At the age of ten, I took a Boy Scout oath, which stated, "On my honor, I will do my best to do my duty to God and my country and to obey the Scout Law; to help other people at all times, to keep myself physically strong, mentally awake, and morally straight." This would go a long way into explaining why I dislike seeing people suffering without at least trying to help, and let it not be said that I failed in my duties, which ten out of ten is impossible. During my childhood and all the way to my adulthood, I hardly ever got into trouble that may be a result of my not doing what I was supposed to do. Nevertheless, I adequately got into situations because I saw things that weren't going right, and I spoke about it without caring about the consequences. Other things that get me into trouble is seeing injustice, unfair treatment, violent, illegal activities, corruption, peoples live getting destroyed, leaders misusing their powers and positions. Discrimination, war, and power struggle—whenever I see any of this happening to people, deep down inside me, it affects and upsets me to the extent that I would be forced to say something because I know that somebody has to say something. And at that point, I don't mind being that person who stood up and went against the grain because human beings have been affected. I know that *hate* is a strong word, but I hate to see helpless babies and kids crying. It kills my heart to see an innocent person being mistreated or crying for help or an innocent person being punished for no just cause.

DPSCS violated all these things. They hurt me and hundreds of other people, and it's unfair. I will not be able to live with myself if I allow DPSCS to continue hurting and destroying people's lives. Happiness is free, but the DPSCS decided not to allow correctional officers who have worked or currently working under their agency to enjoy this one thing that was made free on this planet earth.

As a child, I couldn't tolerate any form of bullying. In school, I often got into a physical altercation with another student, not because the student came to me to look for trouble but because I saw that he or she was beating another student who was helpless and couldn't physically fight back. After fighting the battle for the helpless student, I would walk the student home after school in order to prevent the student from being attacked on his or her way home. Also, when I got to the student's house, I always informed his or her parents the reason why I walked their kid home and what happened at the school. So at this point, after the student made it home safely, people would expect me to go home, right? Okay, but that is not what would happen. Rather than going home, I would turn back and head to the house of the student who I got into a fight with. Most times, I would go past my house and continue going until I reach the bully student's house. When I get there, I would introduce myself to the parents of the student and inform his or her folks what their child did in school and how he or she had bullied somebody else's kid. I would educate the student's parents that they should teach their kid good behavior because charity begins at home. After telling them these things, I would then leave and head for my house. When I get home, my grandmother would ask me, "Who and who did you save today? Which one did you beat up, and which of them did you went over to their place and warn their parents?" Most of the mothers whose children I assisted in school always ended up as friends of my grandmother. On the other hand, the ones that got their kids got beaten by me always came to complain to my grandmother. Anyone who knew me when I was growing up always referred to me as Archangel Michael, defender in the battle. So this had been my life as a child.

During my teenage years in America, I was in one of my class (either student government or science) when a topic was discussed about fishes in Maryland Chesapeake Bay dying and that something needs to be done fast for the ecosystem. I felt bad upon hearing the teacher say those things, and from her tone, I could tell that the fishes were suffering. Without knowing what else to do, when I got home from school, I asked my father how I could send a letter to President Barack Obama in the White House. The letter would address the issue of the Chesapeake Bay fishes that were dying and needing help. After I collected information on how to send a letter to Mr. Obama, I wrote to him complaining and showing my concern about the fishes in the bay. I received a letter from the president that assured me that the fishes in Chesapeake Bay would be protected. The president, through that letter from the White House, informed me of a law that will be in effect that would ban people from throwing things into the bay or in the other tributaries of the bay that could result to the fishes dying. I felt better after reading the response from the president.

Now that both my childhood and spiritual background have been fully established, I will proceed further on what was happening behind the scene. But before that, let me give a quick recap about the revelation that I received prior to this whole problem. Three weeks before the December 19, 2018, death threat note, I felt danger was coming my way. A message was downloaded on my brain. I got information on the names of the officers and supervisors that would try to hurt me in the future and the inmate that they would try to use. I drew step-by-step the role that each one of them would play during the upcoming incident. I prayed about it and asked God to give me the grace to accept the things that I couldn't change and for him to let this incoming storm pass over me if it wasn't meant to pass through me. After crying for four days, I took the names of the officers and supervisors and the steps that they will use to attack me at work. During the three-to-eleven shift, I showed the paper to Lieutenant Michael, explaining to him what is about to happen to me in less than three weeks. I informed the lieutenant that I will confront Major Brian and ask him if I'm still safe in his jail. I also told the lieutenant that I would tell Major Brian about these officers and supervisors that would soon be coming after me. Lieutenant Michael stated the following: "Don't even try it. Do you want to start trouble? How can you report something that hasn't happened yet?" I listened to his advice, but in less than three weeks, my world came crashing down. The good news was that I have lived through the situation because I got myself physically, emotionally, spiritually, and mentally ready for it beforehand. Nothing on this earth could catch me unaware. But back to the behind-the-scene plans to frame me up. Some people might be wondering why I refused to take the outside perimeter wall post on December 24, 2018. Here is the reason why I ran to the DPSCS headquarters for help on January 12, 2018, and also the reason behind my refusal to stay in MRDCC after I got TDY on January 12, 2018, and why I called out sick on January 14, 2018, while working at MRDCC, and why I requested to be transferred back to BCCC after January 31, 2018. Let me start by saying what the two supervisors and officers from the seven-to-three shift were trying to do to me. Captain Donna and Captain Ruth, along with other officers such as Corporal Margaret and Corporal Karen, tried to set me up by planting a contraband inside the state van and making it seem like I did it. This was how they planned it: On December 23, 2018, I was placed inside the Maryland state van. While I was there, I received a warning message that stated, "We will save you today because they are trying to set you up by putting something inside this van. The same people will try to put you on this post tomorrow, but whatever you do, don't step inside this van because tomorrow is the D-day that they have planned. They could be a drive-by shooting. Start to write a letter to Mister Jeffrey, and lastly, make sure you brought that paper that permits you to stay in the front lobby. You are safer in the front lobby as of now. Further instructions to follow."

The same inner voice brought to my attention that "how come it's the supervisors who you wrote up are the ones giving out officers their post on your shift, three to eleven, when they are seven-to-three-shift supervisors? Your three-to-eleven-shift supervisors are working, but seven-to-three-shift supervisors Captain Donna and Captain Ruth took over your shift." I was told to pay attention to my environment and see what is going on. It said, "Things that haven't happened on your shift is happening." The same voice pointed out to me that how come the officers who were sent to relieve me from the van were all seven-to-three-shift officers, the same officers whose friend, Marie, I made a write-up and who all later came after me. The inner voice asked me, "What happened to the officers on your shift? Why can't they be the ones to relieve you?" Behold, on December 24, 2018, the same supervisors ordered me to stay inside the state van. They also told me that my relieving officers were Corporal Margaret and Corporal Karen. I laughed at them and said, "No, my post is front lobby, not outside wall perimeter." I went further into letting them know that I was aware of the setup that they were planning for me by saying, "You people are trying to frame me up by putting contraband inside the state van and pin it on me just like y'all do to other officers. If that's not what you guys are planning, how come I'm being forced to get inside the van? How come you all seven-to-three-shift supervisors are the ones running the three-to-eleven-shift duty sheet while the three-to-eleven-shift supervisors are currently here at work? Also, why is it that my relieving officers are the same seven-to-three-shift officers that have bullied and harassed me nonstop because I wrote their friend up for flirting with an inmate?" After exposing the evil plans they made against me, I then gave the paper that the MRDCC assistant warden wrote that stated that I should be in the front lobby until further notice. From the look in their faces, I knew that they were trying to frame me up.

Similarly, the reason I ran to the DPSCS headquarters for help on January 12, 2018, was because of the warning message that I received while at work on January 11, 2018. Since these supervisors couldn't get me in the state van, they tried another avenue, which was dropping the contraband at the front lobby since everybody knew that the front lobby was my assignment at that time. My inner voice told me to head to DPSCS and explain to them what has been going on and refused to return to BCCC because I will be framed up. I was equally warned against one of the male officers that had been made an offer that he couldn't resist, which was sex. They told me that the officers and supervisors sent him to get information from me and to drop something in my house.

Early in the morning of January 12, 2018, I went to the DPSCS headquarters and explained to the EEO woman what has been going on with me: the discrimination, bullying, harassment, victimization, dehumanization, the setup that they have tried and the ones yet to come. Just like the others, the EEO woman didn't take me seriously. I guess in her mind, she couldn't imagine the possibility of someone being able to see the future events. On the same day, Mister Jeffrey gave me a direct order to report to MRDCC. On my way, I received another warning that updated me on the imminent danger. The warning message said, "Your cutoff time to stay in downtown is 5:30 p.m. Anything after this time, your safety might not be guaranteed. This event will happen after

5:30 p.m., and you are still in downtown. A man wearing a black hoodie with his head covered up will attack you, and you will get stabbed three times on your right side as you are holding the driver's side of the door with your left hand. Leave downtown. Remember, cutoff time is 5:30 p.m." When I got to MRDCC, Mister Jeffrey and Security Chief Mark informed me of my TDY. Afterward, I notified the assistant warden and the security chief that I would like to use my leave hour today because I wouldn't be able to work. Mister Jeffrey asked me why. I told him, "Sir, my cutoff time to be in downtown is 5:30 p.m." Mister Jeffrey thought that I was joking. As he stepped out of the conference room where Security Chief Mark and I were sitting, Security Chief Mark asked me if I can see the future events before it happens. My response was, "Yes, sir. I can see both the past, present, and future." He asked me what I could see about him. I told him all about his past, present, and future. Security Chief Mark stayed away from my case after discovering who I was. He left important information about the division after knowing of my mental ability. Another thing he said to me was, "You are a special being that was born with supernatural gifts."

I started working at MRDCC on January 13, 2018, and before the end of my first day at the jail, the three-to-eleven-shift captain told me that Assistant Warden Jeffrey ordered them to allow me to work by myself without any assistant on 3CM medical unit housing, which has no security camera. When the captain was finished with his message, I asked him this following questions but was never given an answer: "Why would Assistant Warden Jeffrey demand that I work alone in a housing unit that is meant for inmates with mental illness and, on top of that, where there is no security camera? Why would I work by myself in a maximum-security jail when I still have yet to understand the method in which the jail operates on and whose radio communication is way different from my old jail? A new officer is supposed to work with another officer from that jail for at least three days before allowing the new officer to be on their own. Why should my training process be different?" The MRDCC captain repeated himself, saying, "I'm just following the direct order that I received from Mister Jeffrey." Right there and then, I knew that something was cooking and that food wouldn't be served to me. Just like any other reasonable person with common sense, I called in sick on January 14, 2018, the day that the assistant warden wanted me to work by myself, untrained. Moreover, I wasn't about to go down in history as one of the DPSCS correctional officers who got framed up and got sentenced to jail. Nah, I am way too smart for that game.

The way Assistant Warden Jeffrey was playing games with my life and safety, along with the other officers and supervisors, prompted me to request for a transfer back to BCCC in January 31, 2018, when I came back from the hospital. The reason why I wanted to return to BCCC is that the inmates at BCCC at that time couldn't harm me, but inmates at the MRDCC would because those guys don't know me as yet. Another reason why I wanted to go back to BCCC is because the devils that I know are far better than the angels that I don't know. This means that the she-devils that were after me were all on the seven-to-three and eleven-to-seven shift while I was on the three-to-eleven shift. The more DPSCS people ganged up on me to frame me up, the more intense my spiritual gifts became.

During those period, and even until now, the more I pray to God, the more the grace and light he placed on me shone brighter and kept exposing the department. The DPSCS goes to battle with their physical powers, allies, riches, affluence, connections, corruption, intimidation, interference of medical report, false medical documentation, discrimination, dehumanization, victimization, frame-up, and defamation of character. But I, a nobody, comes with the power of the Father, the Son, and the Holy Spirit. I come with all my heavenly warriors. I withstood all the DPSCS attacks and defeated them by the power of the Holy Spirit; the strength that comes from the immaculate heart of the Blessed Virgin Mary; and through the power that was bestowed upon me before I was even born on this earth, my birthright.

DPSCS has hurt and destroyed so many correctional officers' lives. I must give it to them that they also have won many wars through illegal ways. This didn't only make them feel like they are above the law, it also made them more arrogant and cruel toward human beings. It also made them unbeatable. Never in the history of the department did they imagine that their downfall would come from an immigrant correctional officer II with less than five years of service. DPSCS knew that fighting an innocent person is morally, ethically, professionally wrong and it's against the law, but they still enjoy inflicting pain on officers. The DPSCS is filled with arrogance, self-consumed power, wealth, and corruption. They know that fighting an innocent person who has the gifts and glory of God betrothed upon her before she came out on earth is a recipe for the downfall of their division and will expose all its illegal activities.

DPSCS, for the very last time, you all can't destroy something that you can't create. I'm the daughter of the Most High God. Mortals cannot wage war with the immortals. It's just common sense. It's only stupid people that go to battle with God. Men can't fight God. Catch me if you can, DPSCS, after bypassing all the immortal beings in heaven. Additionally, below are the secret weapons that I utilized and are still using to defeat DPSCS.

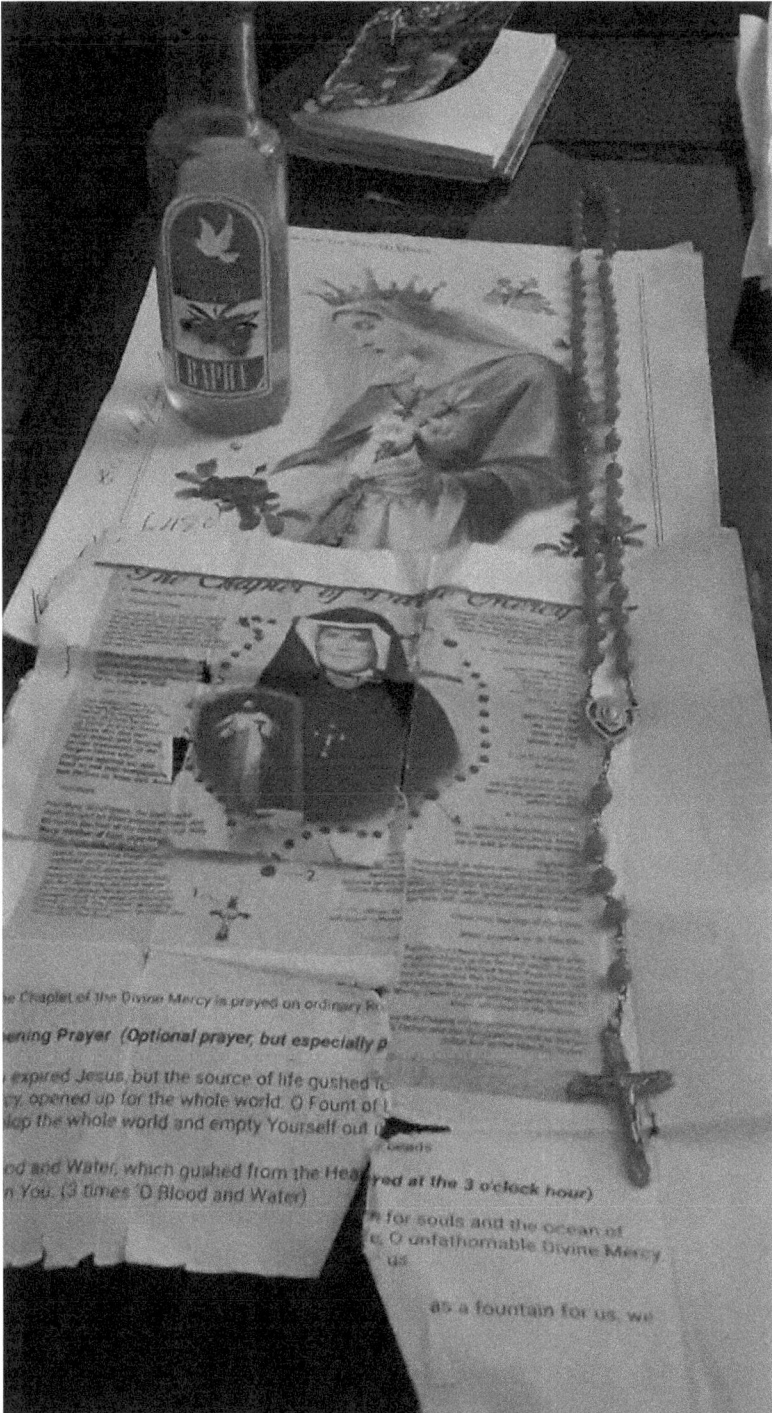

A Prayer to the Holy Spirit

This is the prayer of Pentecost. The Holy Spirit illuminates the human mind and, by indwelling Christ Crucified and Risen, indicates the way to become more like him, that is to be. The image and movement of the love which flows from Christ... (Prayer Pentecost XVI, June 4, 2006)

A PRAYER TO THE HOLY SPIRIT | GOOD NEWS MI

Dear Father, in the name of my Lord Jesus Christ, I ask you to stir up within me the fullness of Your Holy Spirit. Help me to grow in my relationship with the Third Person of Your Holy Trinity and to live in His power and use His gifts.

...whoever is stronger than these three persons may approach my body and my life... so is not stronger than these three Would much better let me be!

Let No Evil Befall Us

O God, You are the preserver of men, and the keeper of our lives. We commit ourselves to Your perfect care on the journey that awaits us. We pray for a safe and auspicious journey. Give Your angels charge over us to keep us in all our ways. Let no evil befall us, nor any harm come to the dwelling that we leave behind. Although we are uncertain of what the days may bring, may we be prepared for any event or delay and greet such with patience and understanding. Bless us, Lord, that we may complete our journey safely and successfully under Your ever-watchful...

5 Powerful Prayers for Protection and Safety

1. Prayer for Personal Protection

Father, I come to You today, bowing in my heart, asking for protection from the evil one. We are assailed moment by moment with images on television, the internet, books and newspapers that leave us vulnerable to sin of every kind. Surround us with Your divine protection. Encompass us round about with Your strength and Your might. Let all who take refuge in You be glad, let them ever sing for joy. And may You shelter us, that those who love Your name may exult in You. For it is You who blesses the righteous man, O LORD, You surround him with favor as with a shield. (Psalm 5:11-12)

...and I ask that You protect our minds. Father, the mind set on the flesh is death, but the mind set on the Spirit is life and peace. (Romans 8:6) O God, set our minds on You. Let us not be conformed to this world, but be transformed by the renewing of our minds that we may prove what Your will is, that which is good and acceptable and perfect. (Romans 12:2) Help us by the power of Your Spirit to think on whatever is true, whatever is honorable, whatever is right, whatever is pure, whatever is lovely, whatever is of good repute, if there is any excellence, if anything is worthy of praise, let our minds dwell on these things. (Philippians 4:8) Strengthen us in the power of Your might. O God, Dress us in Your armor so that we can stand against the schemes of the devil. We know that our struggle is not against flesh and blood, but against the rulers, against the powers, against the world forces of this darkness, against the forces of...

THE
HOLY BIBLE

CSB
CHRISTIAN
STANDARD
BIBLE

HOLMAN
BIBLES

HOLMAN BIBLE PUBLISHERS
NASHVILLE, TENNESSEE

Chinyere Udeh

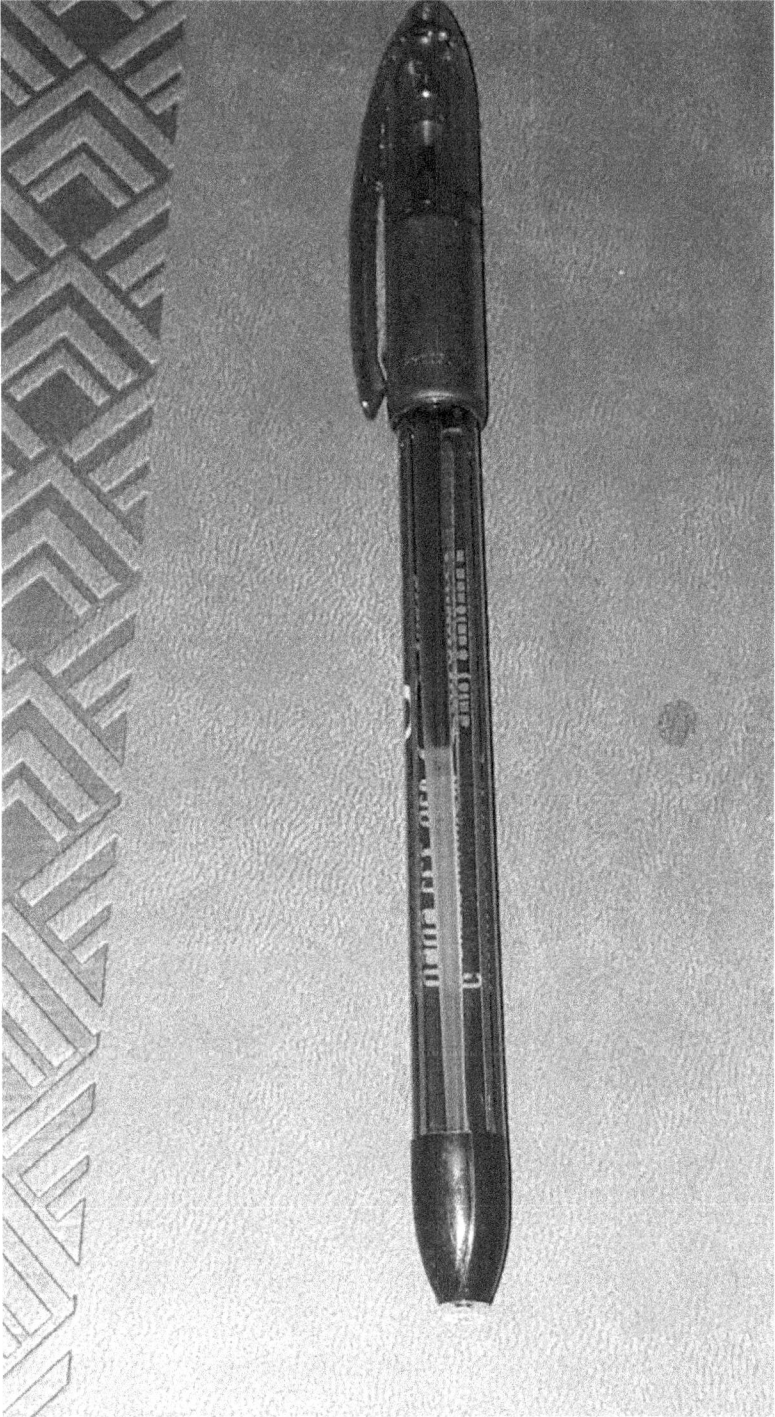

In particular, female correctional officers are sexually exploited—or for a lack of a better word, raped—at the DPSCS by their supervisors, administrators, and upper-ranked officers. My illegal termination from state service was also partly because I refused to be sexually exploited by older men who were old enough to be my father and grandfather. This exploitation has been going on among the female correctional officers, especially the younger ones that are attractive like me. This is based on my experience and observations. Based on my educational background, together with the knowledge that I have, rape is an act whereby a woman did not consent to sex but instead was forced and intentionally placed under duress so that she would comply with the sexual favors that were demanded from her. Furthermore, rape to me is when a woman is under external intimidation wherein she is being forced by an external influence to give her body unwillingly. Meanwhile, there are other factors such as fear of retaliation for refusing to engage in a sexual relationship and fear of being punished for saying no to sexual demands and sex in exchange for protection. Denying of a position as a result of refusing to consent to sex, being victimized, having sex as a result of trying to get something that was meant to be given to them in the first place, encountering physical, mental, and emotional abuse for refusing to engage in sex—all these are what I consider to be rape.

Meanwhile, I have gotten my fair share of top-ranked officers in DPSCS trying to exploit me from 2015 to 2019. But who would I report to? Because at the end of the day, everybody wants the same thing. Because of my personality and unique body type, I became a target for sexual exploitation in the department. Majority of the female correctional officers in the Department of Correction, at one point in their career, are being sexually molested. These officers are afraid to come forward because they all believed that they couldn't fight the system or the government. Also, the fear of being killed, framed up by the department, and other types of retaliation has deterred these innocent victims from telling their stories. The DPSCS claimed that the agency has zero-tolerance policy on sexual harassment. The department wrote the policy in black-and-white to avoid getting in trouble with the government. In reality, there is no such thing as a zero-tolerance policy because the people that made them are the ones that break the law.

On the other hand, there are a few female correctional officers that engage in sex without being forced. They brag about how she had sex with a supervisor or high-ranking official. Disgusting as it might sound, supervisors sleep with four to five female officers on his shift with a promise of giving them a better post to work. As a result of female officers having sex with their supervisors, most of them do not agree to work with each other because of the love-triangle warfare. Also, both supervisors and administrators take their turns in having sex with some female officers by either starting up an issue with a female officer so that the officer would run to the supervisor for help and then give in to his demands. They would also make a promise to the female officer protection or positions, and after they have sex with the officer, they will inform the other men how good it was. The other supervisor or administrator would come for this female officer. This is what most female officers don't know. These female officers don't know that these men are in the same group and are taking turns. Another disadvantage of having sex with the officials, administrators, supervisors is that once the officer starts, she wouldn't be able to stop giving out sex until she unknowingly becomes a public bathroom or gets a disease. The game inside DPSCS is that every younger female correctional officer must have what they call higher-ranked spokesperson, bulldog, and ally. The role of these high-ranking men are to speak in behalf of the female correctional officer on a matter that concerns her. These men would come out to protect this female officer during a time of trouble, giving this officer protection. They also make sure that she gets promoted to a rank she desires even if the female officer is not qualified to be in that position.

Indeed, working at the DPSCS headquarters is equally part of the benefit package that come with having a spokesman, bulldog, and ally. The more bulldogs a female officer has, the more benefit packages she will receive. Knowing that all that glitters are not gold, the price the female officer pays in return is to have sex with these men for positions, protection, favors, etc.

The sexual immoralities that is currently going on and have been going on for years have resulted in the depreciation of DPSCS's values, lack of public trust and respect, increase in corruption, rapidly growing number of lawsuits, inability to meet with federal guidelines, unqualified individuals making unqualified decisions about the interest and affairs of the department, high casualties of correctional officers on duty, decrease in correctional officer employment, and mismanagement of government funding. There are also unethical practices, illegal activities, correctional officers getting killed, increase of contrabands entering the prison facilities, officers being framed up and sent to jail, production of false medical documentation by the department, bad public publicity, and illegal termination from state service.

Going back to my case, the primary reason why I got victimized by DPSCS from 2015 to 2019 was because I didn't have a bulldog, a spokesman, or an ally. I refused to give my body for protection. The most painful part of it all was that during my case, nobody from the DPSCS upper-ranked personnel or anyone from the department that I know stood up to testify on my work ethics and the contributions that I made in the department and also in my punctuality in coming to work and maintaining good working behavior. Nobody said that I go beyond and above to do my job or that I have no disciplinary reprimand or unsatisfactory work performance. I couldn't understand why nobody didn't say or do anything to stop the unfair treatment, discrimination, dehumanization, injustice, and victimization that I encountered. Is it because I am not an American? And if I was a natural-born American citizen rather than an immigrant, would I have been saved? Again, is it because I refused to give out sex in exchange for protection and career advancement? And if I had complied with the department's culture of sex for power, would I have gotten a better treatment and be able to get the case manager position that I qualified for but was intentionally denied from me? If I had dropped my panties down for you all older men with wives and children that might be older than me to get a taste of the forbidden food, would that have made you all not turn a blind eye to the suffering and injustice that were being made to me? Would you know that I'd been innocent all along? Could it had made you all feel more or less than the men that you all are? Or would it have made you all stand up and do the right thing rather than framing me up as being crazy, an endangerment to staff, and unfit to be a correctional officer? Would I have gone through what I went through if I had been your sex toy and bedmate? Would you all bulldogs, allies, and spokesman of DPSCS allow the department to place my pictures all over the downtown Baltimore jails like a common criminal and terrorist, knowing that I was innocent of everything I was accused of? If I would have bent my back, or better still, like I was told, "to suck a dick and bend over," would you all shameless male DPSCS supervisors, administrators, and high-ranking officials sit and watch me being traumatized to the extent that I now need therapeutic treatment as a result of the long-term internalized trauma that I sustained from work-related stress or from being illegally terminated from the state service with no just cause? If I only have given in to the pressure. A wise man in DPSCS once told me that everybody has a price to pay and that I have to pay the price if I want to advance in my career in DPSCS. The department pulled the plug on me by illegally terminating my employment when they discovered that I didn't have money to pay a lawyer who would fight my case, didn't have a bulldog that could come out and save the day, and was not willing to compromise my values.

I began to work at the Chesapeake Detention Facility (CDF), on June 6, 2018. On June 20, 2018, I became a permanent CDF officer.

DPSCS headquarters went in their system and completely changed all my information that was in their database. This DPSCS headquarters' interference of my information worsened the situation of my being underpaid, having lesser leave balance, etc. While I was at CDF, I learned some exciting things that one needed to know about the facility and about the people who are working inside the jail. The CDF is a state building that housed federal detainees and have state correctional officers working there with the federal detainees. Okay, I know that it's somehow confusing, right? Let me break it down further. The federal government leased part of the state jails, in which CDF was one of them, to house their detainees. In other words, federal detainees are placed in the state building together with the state correctional officers.

Let me take you all a step backward when DPSCS headquarters transferred me to CDF against my wishes. During the process of the movement, headquarters failed to inform me that after working in the state minimum, prerelease, and work-release jail (BCCC), maximum-security facility (MRDCC), and being forced on administrative leave on February 28, 2018, that I would be transferred directly to a state building that housed federal maximum security detainees. This was on June 6, 2018. When I got to CDF, apart from the fact that everybody in that jail believed that I was crazy based on the false information they received about me, I was also subjected to work in an environment that I was undertrained for when I was hired as a correctional officer I. I went to the state correctional academy, not federal. The jails that I had worked before were all state buildings with state inmates. So one thing that I didn't understand when I got to CDF was how was it that state correctional officers working in a state building are supervising federal detainees while being undertrained and underpaid? Based on the experience that I encountered while working with the federal detainees and seeing the rate of CDF officers getting hurt by federal detainees, I must say that it was too much. It came to a time when I got tired of hearing 10-13 codes, which meant an officer needed assistance. The longer I stayed in CDF, the more insistent I was for answers about the security issues that needed to be addressed. Again, knowing who I am, I decided to bring the issue to the warden, assistant warden, and security chief of CDF. They gave me their honest opinion, and I respected them for that. I later discovered that the US Marshal oversees the CDF jail and all the decision that concerns the federal detainees. It didn't sit well with me that the US Marshal made all the decisions as to how they want the state to meet the federal standard of housing their detainees without putting into consideration the safety of the state correctional officers who are undertrained and underpaid to supervise the federal detainees. It goes without saying that CDF state correctional officers who were undertrained on how to manage the federal detainees were being forced to work on the capacity of the federal correctional officers, which was realistically impossible.

During that period at CDF, I knew that the jail was risky for all state correctional officers, of which I wasn't an exception. Also, higher expectations of the federal standard were unfairly imposed on state correctional officers at CDF. In my opinion, CDF was a ticking time bomb for the safety of all the officers that were working at the facility. Federal detainees were too aggressive toward the officers, and CDF officers were afraid to put a mace or OC spray on the federal detainees during 10-13 code (officer needed assistance). In CDF, writing up a federal detainee was a waste of time because the detainee will not be punished because they are federal properties. Knowing the detainees' behavior at the CDF, there is a high possibility that one would wonder whether it is the detainees that control the jail and not the correctional officers. These activities made me question again if CDF was safe for any human being to stay in, let alone work in under such an unsafe environment.

Knowing that my life and that of others weren't safe and seeing that none of the DPSCS leaders cared about my coworkers and me and knowing that all they cared about was the money federal government was paying them and not minding the lives and blood of innocent correctional officers that are being shed during prison codes, this situation made me start looking out for my own best interest and that of my fellow correctional officers'. Not minding that these same officers accused me of mental insanity, the first step I took was to have a conversation with the US Marshal who oversaw the CDF jail about the safety concerns I have about the jail. I informed the man that I was undertrained to work with federal detainees and that supervising federal detainee was above the scope of my profession, based on the fact that the academy that I attended was only for state inmates, not federal detainees that are placed in state buildings. Also, I asked him if there is any way CDF officers and I can attend some of their federal training, which would give the officers and me a better understanding of our expectations, how to keep up with the federal guidelines, knowing how to safeguard the federal detainees, and knowing how prevent and deter rapid increase of on-the-job injuries of the officers. The US Marshal was polite and professional. I couldn't recall what he said, but the only thing I got out of it was that I made a good point. For the record, when I got to CDF, the warden made sure that I was shown around the facility, and necessary information were given to me on the same note.

Nevertheless, after my first approach failed, I moved on to the second stage, which was declining to collect or sign for any federal rules, regulations, and standard paperwork given by the supervisors. When I was asked the reason for my actions, I told them that I couldn't take legal responsibility of my actions or inactions toward the way I work with the federal detainees because I needed to be trained at the federal level before taking the legal responsibilities. Let me get one thing straight. I'm not a difficult person to deal with, but I know the type of department that I was working in. These people are coldhearted individuals without any sense of human feelings or sympathy, so I approach them with a lot of diplomacy after mastering their method of operation (MO). Constantly seeing my coworkers getting hurt after trying to reduce the rapid increase in the rate of on-the-job injuries of officers, I started having a third thought about the DPSCS's motives for putting officers' lives at risk and about headquarters sending me to such a place with all the death threats that have been made on my life.

The administrators at CDF as of that time were doing all they could to mitigate these ongoing situations, but from my observation, it was beyond them. There was one day, during CDF's three-to-eleven-shift officers' roll call, when two high-ranking DPSCS officials came to CDF and entered the room where all the three-to-eleven-shift supervisors and officers were doing their roll calls. Initially, when they came in and started talking, there was one question that was in the minds of every officer inside the room. That question was, "Who are these people?" When they finished saying what they were saying and was about to leave, I called their attention by asking, "Please, who are you people? Because by the look of things, neither my fellow officers nor I know." Asking them this question resulted to both of them coming back to introduce themselves to the officers, saying, "We are part of those people in which their pictures are hanging on the walls of every jail's entrance." All the officers were like, "Oh, we don't know that." Seeing those two high-ranking people gave me the opportunity that I was seeking to ask about the officers' safety. When the two officials finished addressing the officers, I raised my hand and said, "Please I have a question." The three-to-eleven-shift captain knew the type of questions I was asking from people, and because of that, he tried to prevent me from asking one of my questions to the two DPSCS high-ranking men. He said, "Miss Margaret Rose, please don't." Every officer in the roll call knows that Margaret Rose's questions are always direct and without filter. Anyway, the officials stated, "Yes, you can ask your question." Then I said, "Okay, my name is Officer Margaret Rose. I was originally from BCCC but was transferred to this jail straight from administrative leave. And upon getting to CDF, I found out that the individuals that were housed here at CDF are all federal detainees. I equally saw that the correctional officers here are getting hurt because of the lack of training of the officers on how to manage federal detainees. Would it be possible that the CDF officers be offered some training on how to manage federal detainees? Could we go to the federal facilities that are run by the federal government to see how the correctional officers there manage their federal detainees and learn from them? Can CDF officers go for in-service training in the federal facilities to learn more about their inmates and detainees since the state academy that all the officers went to didn't cover how to manage federal detainees? Or why can't federal correctional officers come and take care of their detainees that they were trained for while the state correctional officers who are working here at CDF be placed back to the state prison facilities that they have received training for? The reason why I am asking is that federal detainees are different from the state in which I was trained, so I would like to get more training on guarding federal detainees." By the time I finished with all these questions, the whole roll call was silent for two minutes. The two officials, from the look on their faces, weren't expecting to hear such questions; and for that reason, they were not prepared to answer it either. So one of them told me, "Both state and federal are the same, and their detainees as well." In my defense, I said, "Sir, with all due respect, they are not the same. I did my research. Federal government training and requirements are higher than the state, and moreover, federal facilities consist of high-profile individuals with affiliation to white-collar crimes and with highly intelligent detainees and inmates. Unlike the state that has a higher majority of their inmates with handgun charges, drugs, shoplifting, etc." The other DPSCS official stated to me, "So you are that Officer Margaret Rose." I responded, "Yes, sir, I am." My name flew to the DPSCS's high-ranking officials when I broke one of the DPSCS's rules by reaching out to an outside agency for help: I wrote a letter to the governor of Maryland, Elijah.

Meanwhile, after the roll call, all the officers were hugging me, saying, "Margaret Rose, you did good. You gave them a run for their money. We like the way you told them the truth. Now, they will know that all of the correctional officers are not dumb. We get the smart ones." Supervisors, on the other hand, were like, "Margaret Rose, great job at the roll call today. Tell it the way it is."

When I started working in the CDF pods, the detainees were sizing me up to know the type of officer I was. In CDF, they have A, B, C, D, E, and F pods. Inside each pod, there are four different housing units called quarter 1, 2, 3, and 4. Also, each pod has about three correctional officers, and one of the officers must be a sergeant (OIC). Quarter 1 has about 48 detainees, and the same goes for the rest of the quarters for a total of 144 detainees. These detainees are intentionally too demanding, making officers work more than they should. When I noticed their behavior, I told them, "Look, am not going to play that game with y'all. I don't care if you all don't like me, but one thing that I know for a fact is that y'all must obey me. If you don't understand any of my instructions, ask me to repeat, and if you disobey my direct orders, you all will read about it. And for your information, no inmate or detainee under the DPSCS has ever beaten my ticket. If you don't believe me, please try me."

At CDF, I noticed that almost all the detainees don't respect the officers and most of the officers were friends with the detainees. The sad part about it was that both officers and detainees fight for common space. Throughout my career as a correctional officer, I have never allowed an inmate, male or female, or the federal detainees to share a small space with or even come close to me. Again, during my career as an officer, neither state inmates nor federal detainees have ever touched me intentionally or unintentionally. I have always created a healthy boundary and informed them of the consequences that follow such actions. CDF detainees were so much used to squeezing themselves in a tiny space where female officers are standing. A detainee almost tried playing "my body on your body" game with me. Then I turned around, right in front of almost one hundred detainees, and gave him the unforgettable warning of his life. After that day and until I left CDF, none of the detainees tried to do such thing with me again.

Working at CDF made me improve more on my hand-signing language because CDF jail doesn't have an intercom for the officers to use when trying to call for an assistance, plus the radios that they gave the officers in case of emergencies were not working, all the while knowing that the officers supervise federal detainees that are waiting to be sentenced to life imprisonment.

For better understanding, I will go further to illustrate the difference between state requirements for a correctional officer position and the federal correctional officer's job requirements according to the research that I conducted. State correctional institution's requirements include the following: "Be at least eighteen years of age (some states/jurisdictions have a minimum age of twenty-one), possess a high school diploma or GED, have no previous felony convictions, be a United States citizen. Also, possesses a valid driver's license." As for the state correctional's educational requirements, it states, "Although not all agencies require education beyond a high school diploma, some require candidates to possess college coursework in the behavioral or social sciences. Previous law enforcement or military experience is often an acceptable substitute for college coursework. Also, individuals with college degrees or college coursework may be more likely to achieve high-ranking positions within the institution."

In contrast, the federal correctional's requirements include but are not limited to the following:

> Obtained a bachelor's degree. You will need at least a bachelor's degree to work as a federal corrections officer, and one option is a bachelor of science in criminal justice degree program. Such a program typically includes courses in corrections, court systems, and criminal law. You'll also take general education requirements in the four-year curriculum. Addition to that, the training requirement is 120 hours of specialized training at the US Federal Bureau of Prisons. General requirements are candidates must be no older than thirty-six at the time of their appointment unless they have previous experience in a federal civilian law enforcement position, have no previous felony convictions, be a United States citizen. Then again, individuals may qualify for federal correctional jobs if they possess a full, four-year course

of study resulting in a bachelor's degree. Experience requirements in lieu of a degree. Individuals without a bachelor's degree may also qualify for correctional officer jobs if they have at least three years of full-time general experience in one or more of the following areas: assisting individuals, counseling individuals, selling products or services to individuals in a commission-based environment and providing guidance or direction to individuals. In like manner, working in one or more of the following fields: parole/probation worker, juvenile delinquent worker, teacher/counselor, welfare/ social worker, commissioned salesperson, firefighter, emergency medical technician, nurse, and clergyman.

The lies that headquarters, the BCCC supervisors of the seven-to-three shift, the BCCC officers of the seven-to-three and eleven-to-seven shift, and the MRDCC administrators told to the CDF warden, assistant warden, security chief, and the other officers was that I was crazy and unfit to be a correctional officer. Also, that I was a security risk, never came to work, always calling out, no call, no show, refuses to take a draft, complains a lot about her post, causes trouble everywhere she goes, snitch on people, gets officers terminated, sleeps around male officers, and takes female correctional officers' boyfriends from them. Giving credit to where credit is due, I must thank the former warden, Warden Kathy, Assistant Warden Tammy, and current security chief of CDF for not judging me based on the false information they received about me before I came into their jail and also for giving me an opportunity not only in advancing my knowledge while at CDF, but also having the patience enough to understand my work ethics despite all the obstacles and lies that were made up against me by the high-ranking individuals at DPSCS. I was a source of positive contributing factors to CDF throughout my stay. Initially, they thought that I was going to be a liability based on the false information that was passed on to them. On the contrary, I became an asset to them in these areas: custody, traffic, and DNA sampling. While at CDF, I deescalated a massive disturbance of detainees that had a possible chance of escalating into rioting inside the jail by the federal detainees, knowing that the officers were outnumbered. Then again, I aided in stopping a suicidal detainee from committing suicide. As a traffic officer, I took on the responsibility to account for the US Marshal detainees that were housed under the DPSCS in making sure that they are well accounted for and are alive. Clearing of the institutional security count on time and making sure that two detainees who are on different gang are not housed under one cell are equally all part of my duties. When I am not busy mitigating possible security breach or attending duties in traffic, I took on the responsibility of being the DNA collector officer who takes the US Marshal's detainees' DNA samples and sends them to the Maryland State Police Forensic Division for it to be stored in their database. As a DNA collector, avoiding cross-contamination of the detainee's DNA samples, and collecting the sample from the individual that it was made for is my number one priority.

When some of the female officers at CDF saw that what they anticipated didn't happen to me, jealousy began on their side; and before I knew what was happening, they all ganged up against me. Another incident that I ran into while working at CDF (indeed old things, they say, will never change) was that I became fresh meat to one of the male supervisors on the eleven-to-seven shift. By the way, the epidemic of male supervisors requesting or acting to invoke a request for sexual favors from their female subordinate in DPSCS had rapidly grown to the extent that almost every male supervisors believe that they are entitled to have sex with any of the female officers they choose. As I was dealing with these insecure female officers, I was equally encountering discrimination from the DPSCS headquarters. Headquarters were angry at me because I got them in their lies and for not agreeing to say that I was disabled. As a result, they retaliated against me by refusing to give me the job opportunity that I was qualified for. For example, I applied to become part of the intelligence officers who apprehend officers that brings contrabands inside the facility. I was turned down for no reason, and they gave this position to other correctional officers with less criminal justice and investigation skills. Then I applied for the EEO Investigation I position, but got turned down. After that, I asked the headquarters to give me back the case management position that I was qualified for, but was denied by Warden Kimberly. They refused. The more applications that I submitted, the more they all ganged up on me and denied me these positions. DPSCS headquarters told me that I was hired as a correctional officer. I responded to them by saying, "So because I was hired as a correctional officers, does that mean that I have to die as a correctional officer? What happened to the phrase *room for growth?*"

I started applying for jobs outside the state agencies, and I made 100 to 250 job applications outside Maryland, but none of the employers called me for an interview, let alone offer me a job. Furthermore, I went as far as filling up job applications on the NSA job site, FBI, ZipRecruiter, LinkedIn and contacted the career services at my school for jobs, alongside with participating at the university career fairs. After exhausting all these avenues, I knew then that DPSCS blackballed me from getting employment in my field, which is criminal justice. I applied for around 100 to 250 jobs without getting one job out of it. On top of that, I don't have a criminal record, nor am I an illegal immigrant. I'm an American citizen. I have the right to pursue liberty, life, and happiness; but the DPSCS deprived me of those rights because they believed themselves to be above the law and that no one can fight the government or corrupt system. Moreover, the situation of me not being able to get a job after this number of job applications was odd because I have degrees, and I have working experience for those positions that I applied for.

DPSCS headquarters utilized other means to make me feel so frustrated that I will resign from my job. They blocked my number so that I would not be able to reach high-ranking individuals. Headquarters intentionally kept messing with my leave hours, pay increase, paycheck, job opportunities, etc. When I got tired of the constant victimization, I wrote a letter to Governor Elijah, asking him to assist me from the hands of DPSCS on June 18, 2018, and on June 19, 2018, I sent to him this letter.

Dear Governor Elijah,

Governor Larry, your immediate intervention is needed.

Mr. Governor, my name is Margaret Rose. I'm a correctional officer II at the Baltimore City Correctional Center, and I was hired to work as a correctional officer for the Department of Public Safety and Correctional Services on December 1, 2014. So I have been with the Division of Correction for three years and some months now. With this length of years that I have served as an officer is equal to the same number of years that I have been bullied, discriminated, picked on, and dehumanized by my fellow correctional officers at BCCC. Mr. Governor, I'm writing this letter to you because my life and the opportunities that this great country America has offered and has yet to provide is about to be taken away from me. The DPSCS is trying to destroy my life that I have worked so hard for just because I'm an immigrant from a third world country, Nigeria. Mr. Governor, for the past three years of my service, my coworkers from other shifts have created a hostile working environment for me. It all started after I came from the correctional academy in 2015 and also after the event of July 6, 2017, where I witnessed a female officer flirting with an inmate. This officer opened her legs, and the male inmate was standing between her two legs. The officer went forward by touching herself and blowing kisses at the inmate right in front of me. The inmate, on the other hand, was holding his private part. A lot of things happened. But to cut the story short, I reported her to the supervisors and wrote a matter of record. Shortly after that, the female officer and her friends started harassing and intimidating me to go back and rewrite the matter of record that I wrote because they said that what I saw never happened. This event was what made the harassment, bullying, intimidation, and discrimination toward me by fellow officers from the other shifts to increase. For the sake of time, Mr. Governor, I will summarize things for you. However, there is an attached file that will accompany this letter, so hopefully, it will get to you.

Additionally, on Wednesday, July 19, 2017, this officer and her friends came to my post to intimidate me. Also, they tried using inmates to hurt me. I reported these issues to the major and the other supervisors, but nothing was done because the officers in question are all Americans, and I am an African. Sir, it will interest you to know that they have an Africans vs. Americans rivalry in my jail and other prisons as well. Without speculating, Mr. Governor, it means when an African officer is right and an American officer is wrong, the American supervisors will take the side of the American officer who is in the wrong and turn it into the right thing, and the African officer who did the right thing will be turned into wrong.

Moving forward, on May 30, 2017, I was attacked by an ex-inmate at the BCCC at the jail parking lot. Police were called. An IIU officer also came and promised to come back to solve my case, but he never came back. The supervisors and the administrators at the MRDCC covered up the incident.

Sir, please don't forget that I have been bullied, harassed, picked on, discriminated since 2015. I have reported all of them to the supervisors, but nobody did anything to stop the suffering until it escalated to the point when I got a death threat note. On December 19, 2017, I was informed that a death threat had been made on my life by the seven-to-three-shift supervisors Captain Donna and Lieutenant Charlotte. With the same note, Captain Donna told me to sign the death threat note, stating that I don't feel threatened by the death threat note or be moved out of the jail. Again, Mr. Governor, this death threat note was found in Major Brian's mailbox in the administrative area. Sir, inmates are not allowed in the administrative area, only officers and case managers. And the only inmate that goes there, the sanitation worker, is escorted by an officer.

Nonetheless, when I refused to sign my life away, Captain Donna and Lieutenant Ruth, who is now a captain at MRDCC, joined hands with the other officers and increased the level of abuse, intimidation, discrimination, harassment, and bullying that has been happening to me since 2015. I cried every day at work. Then again, on December 30, 2017, Captain Ruth started harassing and discriminating against me again. She abused her power by telling me to change the way I talk and sound before I work at master control so that the American officers can understand me. She picked on my handwriting, calling it a doctor's handwriting. She told me that I don't belong in correction because I'm too nice to be an officer. She said and did a lot of mean and unprofessional things to me. The officers, on the other hand, were calling me "African bitch" and that I should go back to Africa. Sir, I was forbidden from attending the officers' roll call, and my basic human needs and rights were deprived from me, one of which was access to the officers' refrigerator where officers store their foods. Being denied liberty to store my food in the refrigerator resulted in the spoiling of my food. I was eating spoiled food at work every day because I became too hungry and I didn't want to starve myself.

All this happened to me because I refused to sign my life away and to waive liability off the state of Maryland in the event when they finally kill me.

I sent e-mails to Assistant Warden Jeffrey informing him about my working condition. I also requested to be transferred to the headquarters, but nothing was done. I reached out to the headquarters' EEO. Some of the officers told me that the only time DPSCS would let me work at headquarters is when I "suck people dick, bend over, or have a connection." They further told me that my type doesn't belong at headquarters, that the DPSCS will fire me first before letting me work at the headquarters, and it's not all about what I know rather it's about whom I know.

Mr. Governor, the spoiled food that I was eating every day while at work, the harassment, bullying, discrimination, etc. resulted in me passing out while at work on January 31, 2018. I was sent back to my jail, which was BCCC, because I was TDY to MRDCC. When I came back to BCCC, Captain Ruth started picking on me again. She lied on me. Some of the dirty female officers at BCCC told me that I "see too much and say too much." Warden Kimberly tried intimidating me into resigning as a correctional officer, but I refused.

Also, I was told by one of the administrators at MRDCC that I will get hurt or killed if I try to change Correction, because the Correction system is built to be corrupt and that I can't change it. The person added this to his comment: "Your type don't belong here in Correction. Resign. You should be at law school. Be a paralegal or minister of God, but not a correctional officer." The administrator also included in his comment: "We know that you are telling the truth and that you are not the problem, but it's easy for us to say that you are the problem than going to solve the actual problem." The same person told me to be strong mentally because they will come after my mental ability just like they did to others. He said to me, "Be strong, Officer Margaret Rose." Notably, on February 15, 2018, I had another attack while at work, and another 911 was called. What led to this second 911 and ER visit was because I was crying at MRDCC, trying to explain to Warden Kimberly what Captain Ruth and other female officers and supervisors were doing to cover up the officers that wrote the death threat note and who were trying to kill me. But the warden was busy yelling at me just because of the African vs. American politics.

Mr. Governor, in the end, Warden Kimberly, Assistant Warden Christopher, Captain Ruth, Captain Donna, and some other corrupt female officers at BCCC came together and lied to the headquarters, saying that I was crazy and unfit to be a correctional officer just to cover up all the things they have done and still doing to me since 2015. An administrative leave was forced on me by Warden Kimberly and Assistant Warden Jeffrey. I have been on administrative leave from February 20, 2018, till May 30, 2018.

The psych doctor the state sent me for evaluation stated that I wasn't crazy, but he lied on the IQ aspect of his report, and I have proof of this. He based his findings and analysis on an IQ exam that was culturally biased. And as I'm writing to you, the DPSCS are basing their judgment and decisions toward me on a culturally biased IQ exam that the doctor lied about. Also, by law, an IQ exam is not the correct method to use in measuring people's intelligence because of the lack of reliability and accuracy. In addition to this, factors such as culture, genetics, environment, social class, and nutrition can negatively impact a person's IQ exam. Sir, the doctor said that I reason like a fifth grader and that I can't comprehend or make any sentence because of my fifth-grade reasoning. He mentioned in his medical report that I was the cause of my problem and everything that has been happening to me since 2015. The doctor added that I need to self-educate myself into the American culture more because I'm not fully Americanized and that I feel like I'm better than everybody else. Also, he went further in saying that my mathematics skills are at an elementary school level.

So, Mr. Governor, I ask you this question: if I was reasoning like a fifth grader just like the psych doctor said and my comprehension skills are at a fifth grade level, how did I manage to pass the entry-level requirements of a correctional officer? How did I pass the academy and became an officer for three years and some months now? Then again, how did I manage to graduate with honors from Coppin State University, where I obtained a bachelor's degree in criminal justice and a certificate in forensic science? Most importantly, if I was at a fifth grade level, how come I have an associate *degree in law enforcement and correctional administration at the Baltimore City Community College? And presently, Mr. Governor, I'm doing my master's program at American Military University, and the areas that I'm mastering is homeland security and criminal justice. All these academic accomplishments were achieved under three years and six months after becoming a correctional officer.*

Sir, you will not believe what happened afterward. When I got to the headquarters on May 30, Mister Raju and one other woman forced me to say that I have a medical condition. I kept telling them that I don't have a medical condition and that the psych doctor lied, but they gave me a paper that stated that I have a disability just to cover up lies upon lies. Mr. Governor, the most recent event that took place was Warden Kimberly's continuation of the abuse of her powers toward me.

Mr. Governor, out of a passion that I have for the division, it drove me into applying for the case management position. I took the exam and was placed in "better qualified." I waited for an interview, but I was never called for an interview. I will tell you the reason. Warden Kimberly told me right to my face, "You will never become a case manager because you are crazy, and you will let the wrong inmate out." She included the following line: "When you get stabbed by an inmate, that's when the state will pay your medical bills."

Furthermore, it will indeed interest you to know that wardens in each institution play an essential role in selecting who gets promoted and who will become a case manager. Kimberly took advantage of her position as the warden and deprived me an equal opportunity to compete for the case management position by going on an interview since I passed the written examination. Governor, do you know that almost two hundred to four hundred applicants were interviewed for the seventy-five case manager positions? In fact, Westminster requested for additional applicants to fill in their case manager vacancies. Based on Westminster demands, two hundred people were interviewed again. With all these interviews upon interviews, nobody gave me the same opportunity.

Sir, the Declaration of Independence gave me the right to pursue life, liberty, and happiness; but all this abuse of power, discrimination, harassment, unfair treatment, cruel and unusual punishment that I have been going through are in violation of my civil and constitutional rights. Mr. Governor, do you know that I called the Commissioner Mia's office and asked them to help me because of the unfair treatment, the death threat note, and the injustice that Warden Kimberly and others have intentionally inflicted on me for no reason? However, I was told that they couldn't do anything to assist me, then they hung up their phone on me afterward. Please be advised that my medical bills are not yet paid by the state, just like Warden Kimberly told me. Also, the only thing that is remaining to happen to me is getting stabbed by an inmate since everything Kimberly said to me has already happened.

Sir, please, I need your help since everybody is covering up for each other. The only crime that I have committed so far is being an immigrant. Mr. Governor, I don't have a connection like Warden Kimberly. I'm not an American like her, nor have power or money. Instead, I'm a poor immigrant from a third world country who came to America for a better opportunity and who firmly believes in the American justice system. Please give me justice. Save me before I get killed in DPSCS. Mr. Governor, I might not have what Warden Kimberly and every other person who has been intimidating me and covering up the truth has. The only thing I have is honesty and integrity. Sir, please don't believe anybody that will tell you that my matter has been resolved because that's a lie. I wouldn't be e-mailing you, asking for your help if this issue has been resolved. Sir, my medical bills are critical to me. Please help me before DPSCS destroys the life that I have made for myself here in America—the land of freedom, opportunity, and the home of the brave. Or they might even kill me, just like they stated in the death threat note. I'm indeed in fear for my life. Mr. Governor, you are my last hope. Please help me.

From a correctional officer, Margaret Rose

June 18, 2018

On July 2, 2018, after DPSCS received the letter that I sent to the governor, I received a letter from Nicole, management associate from the office of the secretary of the state, restating back all the victimization treatment that I was getting from the department without offering any assistance or solution.

On July 6, 2018, I responded to Nicole, inquiring why she restated the issues of victimization and discrimination that I wrote to the governor without offering any help or solution that could remedy the ongoing problem. Nicole didn't respond to the last matter of record that I sent through the CDF former warden until today.

Thinking that DPSCS, after reporting them to the governor, would leave me alone and find someone else to pick on, they didn't. Instead, the level of victimization rapidly grew. At that point, I was left with no choice but to report them to the EEOC; and on July 31, 2018, I signed the EEOC discrimination charge paperwork against the Department of Correction.

Not surprisingly, DPSCS retaliated against me for placing a discrimination charge against them. The EEOC discrimination charge that I signed against DPSCS mysteriously got compromised, and DPSCS was never held accountable for what they put me through from 2015 to 2018. DPSCS looked for different ways to illegally terminate me, but I never gave them the reason. It was later that somebody told me I was blackballed from getting any employment in the United States in general. Knowing how corrupt DPSCS is, their illegal attempts to fire me, countless number of death threats on my life, and interference of my information in their database, I couldn't underestimate them. In my opinion, I was blackballed.

With all these things were going on, I was confronted by female correctional officers at CDF inside the facility elevator and work phone. They all accused me of trying to take their correctional officer boyfriends from them. These officers didn't just stop there; they started sharing my personal information to the detainees. My safety got compromised when CDF officers informed their detainees the type of handgun I bring to work and that I store it inside the master control center alongside with other officers who bring their guns to work. Detainees at CDF are locked in their quarters and don't have access to come out in the front lobby let alone go inside the master control center. As a result of this and many other safety issues that I encountered, I again asked to be transferred to the headquarters on October 21, 2018. The transfer that I requested for was never made, but with the help of the former CDF warden, Warden Kathy, I was able to get a position as project manager and statistic data analyst at DPSCS medical department. Under Chief Joseph, I was to assist in making sure that the department is following the federal government guidelines on the detainees' medical and housing conditions.

The Duvall, et al. settlement agreement lawsuit case (1:94-cv-02541-ELH Document 539-1 Filed 12/14/15 in the United States district court for the District of Maryland (Civil Case No. 1:94-CV-02541-ELH) was another case that I participated in.

I left CDF in the end of October and went to Jail Industries Building (JI) at 531 E. Madison St. Baltimore, Maryland, 21202, where I started work. Upon starting the job at the Jail Industries Building in November 2018, I encountered Major Angela, who oversaw the JI Building. Angela immediately started harassing and bullying me because of the civilian clothing that I was wearing. She believed that as a junior officer, I was supposed to be in uniform rather than in civilian clothing while working at the office. After I got the position as a medical department project manager and statistic data analyst, CDF Warden Kathy and Chief Joseph both agreed that it would be professional if I go on civilian clothing rather than uniform because of my current position. So that was how I came about wearing the civilian clothing, which Major Angela found offensive. As I was working at JI Building, Major Angela kept making racial comments toward me. Some of her statements include, "This one gets to go. She doesn't belong here. She is different." That's the comment that Angela makes every time she sees me or when she walks past my office. Additionally, Major Angela encouraged almost all the officers at the commissioner's house to start harassing and bullying me. She also ganged up with these officers, and they started calling me crazy. Both Angela and the officers at the commissioner's house was telling Mister Thomas, the deputy commissioner, to send me back to the CDF. Major Angela didn't stop the madness of instigating all the female correctional officers at the commissioner's house to harass me. She also convinced them to join her in complaining about the civilian clothing that I was wearing to work. Again, they all teamed up and started to create an unnecessary problem of me being off the uniform. Major Angela confronted Chief Joseph, my supervisor, demanding to know why he allowed me to be in civilian clothing. Meanwhile, when Mister Thomas got tired of the female officers talking his ears off, he ordered me to return to wearing my uniform. Letting peace reign, I went back to wearing my uniform while still working as the project manager and statistic data analyst. Thinking that Major Angela and her group would let me be, they still kept harassing me every time I came to the commissioner's house to present and explain important information on how the medical Duvall settlement agreement lawsuit was progressing and some of the barriers in the case. The officers made it known to me that a nobody like me doesn't sit next to the commissioner. They gave me a direct order to sit way at the back. Sitting where I was ordered to sit made it difficult for Mister Thomas and the others to understand the information that I was trying to pass on to them. I did all this so that the commissioner will see that I'm not crazy and I'm not a troublemaker. The information they got about me was that I start trouble everywhere I go and that trouble follows me. Also, knowing that the CDF warden went out of her way to help me talk to the man that gave me the job, I didn't want to disappoint her or to be ungrateful to the man who gave me an opportunity that DPSCS intentionally refused me.

As I was working at JI Building, headquarters blocked my cell phone from making calls to anyone in DPSCS. Other normal things that an officer was entitled to were denied to me. With the help of Mister Thomas and Chief Joseph, headquarters unlocked my phone but never gave me all my entitlements. At JI Building, I was the only one in the office that doesn't have the Internet on her computer and whose office phone wasn't working. After putting many tickets for a maintenance request, nobody showed up to fix my desktop computer, the Internet issue, or my office phone.

DPSCS headquarters did all they could to send me back to the CDF, believing that I would be asked by Chief Joseph to go back when I couldn't do the job that they hired me to do because of the Internet issue. Not letting anything to get in my way, I implemented a new method that countered Major Angela and her headquarters friends who were trying to sabotage my new position by denying Internet services on my work computer. I started bringing my laptop to work. The Internet connection that I was using in my office came from the hot spot of my T-Mobile phone. When Major Angela saw that her plan failed, she started attacking Chief Joseph. Major Angela never knew that I have already gotten permission from Chief Joseph and received DPSCS guideline policy on how to bring personal laptops inside the state property from the department technology help desk. And of course, common sense already told me what type of information to research on a personal computer and the ones that are not. To show how committed I was with my job, I would always go back to CDF three-to-eleven shift to use the state computer anytime my assignment entails confidential information about the detainees. Headquarters was so focused on making my life miserable that they lost sight of the fact that I was assisting the state to avoid paying for the settlement lawsuit money.

While at JI Building, I received an august visitor around the end of November and the beginning of December. The DPSCS internal investigator visited me. The IIU investigator came to interrogate and harass me. The investigator accused me of being the one that has been causing all the problems that are happening at DPSCS. He yelled at me in my office as if I was a criminal, but I was the victim.

Let me share a light on this IIU encounter. On May 30, 2017, when an ex-inmate of BCCC attacked me, DPSCS Internal Investigation

Unit was informed about the incident. An investigator was sent after one month. When the investigator came, he promised to come back and solve my case. He never came in 2017. Another incident occurred, which was the death threat note on December 19, 2017. However, I reached out to the Internal Investigation Unit for help on January 12, 2018, and got turned down. After a year, six months, and some weeks that I encountered that major life-threatening attack, DPSCS IIU finally sent their investigator, but he interrogated and accused me of being the cause of all the DPSCS ongoing issues instead of helping me figure out why I was being targeted in the department. After one year, six months, and some weeks, DPSCS IIU investigator came to my office at JI Building and yelled at me for reaching out to them. Not minding who the investigator was who sent him and who he was representing, I yelled back at him and told him to leave my office. He got mad and left. Feeling the way he did, he lied in his report. At this point, I didn't care anymore because everything about the department are all lies. He closed my case.

With the help of the DPSCS headquarters and officers from the commissioner's office, Major Angela finally got her way by sending me back to CDF on January 11, 2019. I got away from BCCC's victimizations, discrimination, dehumanization, and their ganging up on me. Also, I overcame the two attempts that were made on my life at MRDCC. Then I stayed away from the CDF female officers' drama and sought refuge at the JI Building. Just as I was about to put my life back together, Major Angela came in and started her discrimination. Major Angela sent me back to the same CDF where I encountered hostile work environment, sharing my personal information to the federal detainees by the officers, officers calling me crazy and a snitch, and some female officers ganging up on me.

Both Warden Kathy and Assistant Warden Tammy had retired by the time Major Angela sent me back to the CDF. When I arrived at CDF, I saw the new warden, Warden Rebecca. I tried explaining to her about my ongoing situation of being victimized by the officers, the harassment, together with the ganging up of the officers and bullying. Warden Rebecca refused to reason with me, just like Warden Kimberly refused to listen to me before she supported the Americans. Knowing that I will never undermine my safety for anything, I notified the warden about the matter of record that I wrote on October 21, 2018, before leaving for the JI Building. I informed her that I would like to be transferred since Warden Kathy never granted my transfer before I left for the JI Building. Again, she refused to understand or reason with me. Knowing that she is a new warden who is trying to gain the approval of the DPSCS headquarters in exchange for my life, I visited Mister Thomas at the commissioner's house. When I got there, I saw that the deputy commissioner, Mister Thomas, was busy, so I spoke to a lady. Initially, the lady, Mister Thomas's personal aid, and the commissioner of the pretrial all thought that I was still at the JI Building under Chief Joseph, my direct supervisor. Getting the surprise of their lives, neither Chief Joseph nor any of the high-ranking individuals knew or approved of Major Angela sending me back to the CDF. I was crying while explaining to the woman at the commissioner's house the suffering that I went through since 2015 up to the present day. As I was crying, the woman noticed that I was not breathing very well, so she offered to call an ambulance for me, but I refused. I later went back to the CDF. When I got there, Warden Rebecca placed me on full paid administrative leave. When I requested to know why she is sending me on administrative leave, she said the following: "You will be on administrative leave until we can find where to transfer you to." She gave me a direct order to call her on the phone every day from Monday to Friday between the hours of 9:00 a.m. to 10:00 a.m.

Meanwhile, I was able to come up with some theory findings that could resolve the Duvall settlement agreement lawsuit. I also discovered an unforeseen statistical danger in the decrease rate of correctional officers and workers at the DPSCS in the year 2025. Unfortunately, I wasn't able to share the theory findings with the DPSCS leaders because Major Angela and her headquarter friends, together with the others at the Commissioner Thomas's office, sent me back to CDF. These people believed that my type, an immigrant, shouldn't be working with the commissioner. If these theory findings were to be carried out, it will not only resolve the Duvall settlement case that the state of Maryland is currently facing, it will also reduce the rate of lawsuits that the state of Maryland is facing from the correctional officers. Also, it will increase the percentages of hiring and retaining correctional officers. The theory findings will enable the DPSCS to meet and exceed the federal guidelines of housing inmates/detainees. Also, instead of the forecasted depreciation of the officers by the year 2025, it will raise those numbers three times. And because of that, the department will not only make more revenues, while maintaining beyond maximum numbers of state correctional officers that work under DPSCS, but will also cut down on the overtime spending.

Here is a quick recap about the Duvall settlement agreement lawsuit, alongside my suggested solutions:

> The responsibilities of the monitors shall be to (a) conduct on-site inspections of BCDC as necessary in their professional judgment to monitor the implementation of this settlement agreement but no less frequently than once every six months for the first two years from the effective date and (b) review evidence relating to compliance and assess the commissioner's progress in meeting the requirements of this settlement agreement, including assessing any allegations of the plaintiffs regarding lack of compliance.
>
> Attorney's fees and costs: (A) Defendants shall pay plaintiffs $450,000 in full and final satisfaction of all claims of plaintiffs for attorney's fees and costs in connection with this auction before the effective date. (B) Plaintiffs shall be entitled to reasonable fees and costs of monitoring compliance with the substantive provisions of this settlement agreement in an amount not exceed $30,000 per year in the first and fourth years following the effective date and $20,000 per year in the second and third years following the effective date.

After reading, analyzing, and articulating the settlement of agreement, I came up with an example together with a solution for this ongoing lawsuit issue. For example:

Settlement Agreement Theory Findings

To resolve the adverse working conditions of the correctional officers, the strategic approach that will assist in facilitating good working condition for the officers and their motivation and willingness to come to work and do their job as well as in resolving the settlement agreement lawsuit include the following:

1. Reexamine the leadership structure of the DPSCS and eliminate the corrupt individuals who are poisoning and corrupting the system. Beginning from the headquarters' manager of employee relations unit, the state medical directors, DPSCS independent psychological evaluation doctors, and down to the least corrupt supervisors in the department.

2. Stop victimization and mistreatment of officers. Treat correctional officers fairly, firmly, and impartially.

3. Extend a little kindness and compassion to the officers by treating them like human beings.

4. DPSCS should know that everything is not always about money.

5. Most importantly, supervisors, administrators, and headquarters need to stop taking issues on a personal level; rather, all situations should be treated professionally. When DPSCS headquarters gets their feelings involved, they make a criminal act against the officers by using their positions to frame officers up. Most times, supervisors, administrators, officers, and headquarters label officers crazy and unfit. They go as far as producing a false medical report from the state medical doctor to support their lies. Most of the time, officers get illegally fired either framing by planting

contraband on the officers' area or creating a false medical result.

6. Give opportunities to immigrants inside the Department of Correction. DPSCS has a doctorate honor in discriminating immigrants, especially Nigerians. For instance, 99.9 percent of the individuals that are working at the headquarters are all Americans. Hardly would one see an immigrant working at the DPSCS headquarters. It goes without saying that immigrants have acquired educational skills and experience needed to be able to hold positions, but they are still socially disenfranchised as a result of the DPSCS discriminatory nature toward immigrants.

7. Correctional officers need to be motivated by giving them reasons to want to get up from their beds, leave their homes, and come to work.

8. Correctional officers wish to be appreciated, not to be crucified. They wish that the department could be more encouraging, not corrupt, and be more culturally diverse rather than being culturally biased. Furthermore, the officers hope for tuition reimbursement and encouragement from the department for them to become a better version of themselves rather than being enslaved to work and being overly drafted. Officers want their leaders to have integrity, not to be intimidated them. They pray to be treated with respect and not being retaliated.

9. Correctional officers want to gain experience, not be exploited. They are looking to become successful in their career, not to engage in the sexual act during their career for protection and promotion. Officers want the department to treat them with fairness and not be illegally fired. They want the leaders not to frame them up rather to be firm.

Officers don't want to be blackballed from getting another job; instead, they want the DPSCS to give them an opportunity.

10. Officers want to work in a peaceful working environment, not a hostile working environment. Correctional officers would like to be treated like human beings, not being dehumanized by the very agency they are working for. They want their voice to be heard, not be ignored. Correctional officers want to work, but not be overworked. They need motivation from the system, not for the system to destroy what they have accomplished. Officers want the system to be corrected, not corrupted. The DPSCS should show a little care and kindness to the officers because it could go a long way to change the mind-set and behavior of an officer toward his or her job. Just a little bit of kindness toward the officers.

These are some of the ways to resolve almost all the problems that are making officers not wanting to do their job, which in turn have affected both medical and dietary aspects of every jail in the Department of Correction, and that includes the Baltimore Central Booking and Intake Center, the origin of the Duvall settlement agreement lawsuit case. These are the things that will change if the DPSCS leaders agree to go with my suggestions:

1. Decrease of lawsuits by correctional officers.
2. Decrease of victimization made to the officers by DPSCS headquarters.
3. The rebuilding of public reputations of the department.
4. There will be room for career growth and to be culturally diverse.
5. Increase in employment and retaining of the correctional officers currently employed.

6. Reducing corruption and the introduction of contrabands in the prison facilities.
7. There will be no such thing as officers being framed up or having false medical documentation from the state medical doctors.
8. The issue of Duvall settlement agreement lawsuit case and any other lawsuit will be resolved.

An important fact to remember: correctional officers are human beings. They are not aliens, nor did they drop from the sky. The point that I'm trying to make is that officers have family members, friends, and relations that they share their sad stories about, like how they are being treated at work, together with how the system doesn't care about them since they can't disclose such information to the media because it will be a breach of contract. As you all might not know, the reason why correctional officers do not reach out to outside resource or come forward to the news stations is because of the nondisclosure contract we all signed before going to the state academy. Failure to uphold the DPSCS code of silence and secrecy will automatically get an officer fired from state service, get blackballed for life, and get the correctional officer killed. Yes, you all heard me correctly. Yes, an officer will get killed when they stop keeping the code of silence and secrecy. Some of them get framed up and end up in prison. Majority of the time, bad things happen to the officer while serving the prison terms under the Department of Correction.

Let me go further to explain on how dangerous it is for someone to break the code of secrecy and silence inside the DPSCS like I'm comfortably doing right now. The Department of Correction is so corrupt that they don't care about killing any human being who stood in their way of protecting their dirty secrets. The DPSCS leaders and headquarters see correctional officers as bodies that can disposed of at any given time, as paychecks, and as a statistic. These people don't consider officers as human beings like them, and that makes it more dangerous for any officer under the department who decides to go against the grain.

Now people will begin to wonder how come I'm still alive since I broke the code of silence. Well, the truth of the matter is that more than five death attempts have been made to my life. All were unsuccessful. DPSCS didn't succeed in killing me or framing me up as they did with the other officers. The reason was that DPSCS was not as strong as they look when it comes in destroying something that they couldn't create. Another reason was that they would be held accountable by law if anything were to happen to me as a result of the numerous attempts they have already made on my life. DPSCS would be the prime suspect, and that was one attention they didn't want. Next was because they were confused about the type of person that I am. They haven't seen anyone who isn't afraid or gets intimidated by them.

Anyway, the last attempt I had was in connection with my car. Somebody intentionally took out all the front driver's side bolts off the tire. To cut the story short, I was driving around the city with a car with the driver's side tire almost coming out without my noticing it. As I was driving one day, all of a sudden I started feeling a high intensity of danger right in front of me. After that came a warning command that gave me instructions. Just to clear the air, the downloads that I receive in my brain are always given to me in a step-by-step instruction. Also, the downloads equally provide me the reason why I should do to what I was being asked to do and what would happen if I don't follow the instruction and the consequences of not following the information given. In addition to this, the downloads of the information in my brains give me direction on the specific things to do, precisely where to go, whom to talk to, what to say, what not to say or do, assignment limitation, what time to leave wherever I was sent to. The information I received while driving said the following: "Don't go on the beltway, don't drive fast, drive slow, and get to the nearest auto shop. If you try to drive fast, your driver's side tire will come out and you will lose total control of this car. Keep driving because you have a limited time, but we will make sure you get there safe. Time is running out." I was getting this uploaded information while I was still driving. When I got to an auto shop, I informed the man to check my driver's side tire to know what was wrong with it. After the auto repairman lifted my car, which I was watching him do, he said this: "Did you drive this car here? And if yes, how did you manage because your driver's side tire is almost completely out. Where did you take your car last?" I, on the other hand, responded, "I just got the car new, and it has passed both MVA inspections together with the Maryland emission test. And the car has not gotten fixed by anyone since I bought it four to six months ago. You are the first auto repair I took this car to." I left the place after the man helped me with the tire. This incident took place five days before the fact-finding conference meeting I was supposed to attend with DPSCS at the office of the Commission on Civil Rights on August 15, 2019.

Currently, DPSCS is the only one who have a motive to harming or killing me because of the following reason: For many years, the department has been intimidating, illegally terminating officers, and victimizing them. They got away with it because that's how they make correctional officers scared. DPSCS headquarters and their leaders go about treating people like they are nothing. They never imagined that a day would come when an officer will rise and defeat them in their games using their method. It's like a bruise on their ego. Smart but dumb, as they all are, headquarters unintentionally exposed me to the deep secret of how corrupt the agency is when they used their technique of firing officers on me. Unfortunately for them, by the time they recognized what they have done, it was too late because I had already become a master in their own game. Not only was I a master, I also gained insight on how bad things happen to the correctional officers. Headquarters was scared having me in the department because of the amount of information I obtained that wasn't meant for me to know. DPSCS knew that I was going to tell on them. They saw me as a threat, so they wanted to get rid of the threat by any means possible.

For your information, those correctional officers that were being shown on TV that were accused of committing crimes were all innocent. Because with the level of corruption that is happening inside the DPSCS, anybody could be framed up and sent to jail once the headquarters see the individual as a threat. Don't believe every news that you all hear about the state of Maryland correctional officers because nine out of ten, the officer is innocent but has no money to get a lawyer.

Anyway, back to what I was saying about correctional officers passing information about their working conditions to their families.

These correctional officers' families, relatives, and friends also have their own group that they pass the same information to. And like they said, bad news travels faster than good news. The rapid rate of the corruption in the Department of Corrections is one of the main reasons why people don't want to work in the department as a correctional officer no matter how much money you pay them. Nobody wants to be framed up for a crime they didn't commit or go to jail because of it. However, with these positive changes that I have suggested to the department, it will assist in raising back up the number of correctional officers working at the department.

Acknowledging the fact that the governor of Maryland gave 10 percent salary increase to all the state correctional officers, the officers appreciated his generosity. But with all due respect, Mr. Governor, there are things money cannot buy, and those are the things almost every correctional officer are asking for from the DPSCS headquarters. Officers want to be treated like human beings, not to be discriminated against, to trade off sex for protection or promotion, etc. On the other hand, if DPSCS disregards the theory findings and suggestions, the number of their officers will decrease rapidly. They would not be able to meet the federal guidelines on housing inmates and detainees. Again, at the rate DPSCS are going with their illegal activities against the officers, thinking that there are above the law; the injustice that is being made by the officers; the blood of innocent correctional officers who have been killed in and outside the jails; blood of inmates, detainees, and officers during 10-13 code; the corrupt system; and discrimination, dehumanization, and victimization of officers that have stained the department. The DPSCS will not be able to make it to the year 2025 because of the numbers of correctional officers dropping every year.

The Duvall settlement agreement was a wake-up call to all the DPSCS leaders regarding the level of damage the headquarters, supervisors, administrators, and the corrupt system have created for the correctional officers, to the extent that they are just in for the money rather than doing their job. It's time to stand up for change, a time to say no to discrimination, time to offer officers career advancement without sexual exploitation. Finally, it's time for the Department of Corrections to do the right thing for once.

With the increase of corruption and victimization of correctional officers at the DPSCS, it will be hard to bring the employment of the officers up in the year 2025 if change doesn't occur.

If the department works on the areas of corruption, dehumanization of the officers, frame-up, illegal termination, career advancement, etc., then by the year 2025, there will be a big change in the hiring and retaining of correctional officers.

Another behind-the-scene event that happened was three weeks before I was sent on administrative leave by the new CDF warden, Rebecca. On December 2018, around the middle week, I went to the commissioner's office, which was located at the O'Brien House, in search of personal immunity protection that will protect me from being framed up, victimized the second time, headquarters making another illegal attempt to fire me from the state service, or undergoing another dehumanization treatment from DPSCS. So when I got to the O'Brien House, I requested to speak to any of the commissioners or to the deputy commissioner, Mister Thomas. Unfortunately, I wasn't able to see either of them. However, I saw a lady that I spoke with in regard to getting some immunity protection from the upcoming incident. The main reason I went to the commissioner's house was for me to prevent that incident from happening. Without putting any blame on the woman, the lady was confused about what was going on and why I was requesting for protection against something that hasn't happened yet. So as not to make me look weird, which was nice of her, she asked me if I was being harassed, threatened, or being bullied recently. My response to her was, "No, but will soon be victimized and lied to the second time. An upcoming conspiracy incident against me by the department is coming closer to me. Please, I want to prevent it from happening again. History is about to repeat itself, and this time, I will not be able to fight them off because there are many of them, and all of these people are women. Some will be coming from headquarters while the rest came from the jails, all females." Nevertheless, the lady politely told me that the commissioner doesn't grant immunity for an event that has not yet happened. She was honestly trying to make sense of what I was saying, but she couldn't. Well, I later left the O'Brien House and went back to the JI Building. So three weeks after my visit to the commissioner's house, Major Angela sent me back to the CDF, which then resulted in this second victimization from DPSCS.

The lady I saw three weeks ago was the same person I met on January 11, 2019, when I came back to the commissioner's house to know the reason why the major sent me back to the CDF. This issue would have been prevented three weeks before the actual incident occurred. Well, I didn't blame her for not taking me seriously because not everyone will understand the gifts that God gave me. The ability to see the future or upcoming event before it happened was part of the gift package that I was born with. Furthermore, as I was on administrative leave, Warden Rebecca and Miss Pamela started threatening and harassing me that they will make me lose my job. These two women began forcing me to undergo another medical evaluation for fitness for duty because they accused me of being unfit. Knowing that this is the method DPSCS utilizes in illegally terminating officers, coupled with the first experience I had with them and their state medical doctor, made me invoke my Fourteenth Amendment right (right to refuse or accept medical treatment). In my case, I refused to go back the second time for medical evaluation that I never requested. Warden Rebecca's and Miss Pamela's constant harassment made me believe that DPSCS headquarters was on their best bullshit again and they were up to something. Knowing that I was about to get terminated illegally from the state service, it motivated me to start making videos of what was going on with me and share it to the public, together with educating correctional officers on the level of corruption that is being conducted inside the DPSCS. I made more than ten videos and provided documentation to prove to the world that what was happening to me was real and that it wasn't just a Facebook fun. I posted all the information on my Facebook page. The other aim I had before making the videos was to get the attention of the DPSCS high-ranking leaders because headquarters blocked my phone number and e-mail address again so that I could not call or write to them, so social media was my last option at that time. Almost all the correctional officers were worried that I would get killed by the DPSCS because nobody has publicly called them out for their corruption. They were scared for my life. I, on the other hand, didn't care because I felt that somebody had to lay his or her life down so that others will live.

I didn't mind being that person because officers were suffering. Also, even knowing that the DPSCS code of secrecy and silence forbade the correctional officers from reaching out for help from an outside source, I still didn't care. I knew that somebody has to stand up for a change. I also knew that it was time for me to rise and shine my light. I knew that the hour has come for me to get up and protect the only thing that matters to me, which are the human beings. It was the time for me to live up to my duty of protecting humanity.

During that dark period in the department, when the leaders no longer valued human lives, it was the perfect time for me to pick up the call. I answered to the call that brought me to this earth, which is to help humanity. I have always known that for me to come out of my mother's womb with these gifts given to me by God, it means that I was to use them to help others during the darkest time. Officers were scared that the Internal Investigation Unit of the DPSCS would arrest me. Others believed that I would get killed, and few thought that I would get fired for posting videos about the department on Facebook. The truth of the matter was that, I encountered a lot of death threats before and after the videos. I got illegally terminated—not directly because of the videos that I posted but indirectly. Let me explain. DPSCS policy states that correctional officers can't talk to the media (newspeople), but there is no provision that prohibits officers from posting videos about the illegal activities that are going on in the department on his or her social media page. When the DPSCS made their policy, social media like Facebook wasn't in existence, so they thought that it wasn't necessary to include it. After Facebook became in use, none of them bothered to include it in their policy, and because of that, I wasn't in violation. All of them were too smart on how to come up with ways to frame officers up and produce false medical reports from their fake doctors, but ironically, they were too dumb to know that social media travels faster than the news media, and people all over the world have access to their social media news than the normal TV news media. After explaining to the officers the pros and cons of the media policy of the department, officers started posting on their Facebook page the issues that they were undergoing in the department. Correctional officers learned a lot from my case because I made it available for them to see and learn through my Facebook page.

Meanwhile, I received messages from almost all the correctional officers that work for DPSCS telling me that they are standing up for the same change that I speak of but were too afraid to come out as bravely as me.

Some people might be asking me whether risking my life and losing the only source of income worth the fight. The answer to that question is yes. If only you all can be in my shoe and feel the pain I went through from 2015 to 2019: nonstop victimization, dehumanization treatment, being framed up, intentionally depriving of job opportunities, etc. If you all could witness the inhumane treatment, injustice, and the level of intimidation and retaliation and see the blood of innocent correctional officers that are being wasted every day inside the institution and the magnitude of the victimization officers goes through from the headquarters. Some officers have given up hope of DPSCS being better. Some officers have been made to believe that they are less than human beings. Officers are suffering inside the department in silence. We have great correctional officers who have invested thirty years of their life in the service. Additionally, officers are being framed up and sentenced to prison for a crime they didn't commit. Others are being accused of mental instability and being unfit for duty, and as a result, the department fires them illegally for no reason. Good officers have turned into dirty officers. Female correctional officers are giving up their bodies for protection and career advancement. Officers' innocence are stolen from them. And the majority of the officers can't even express their feelings very well in writing let alone fight for themselves. Others have been brainwashed to fear the corrupt system more than the God who created them. So my answer again is yes. I don't mind giving up both my life and career to save millions of victimized correctional officers who are currently facing the same obstacles. Again, I don't mind losing everything that I have worked for in an exchange of preventing another innocent correctional officer who is still in the academy from going through a life-changing experience that I went through starting from 2015 until 2019.

The only way people can understand the reason why I have chosen to give up everything to save almost everybody is to first walk in my shoes and feel my pain and, second, if you are or were a correctional officer or if you have a relative who is or was an ex-correctional officer, etc. When DPSCS headquarters saw that the method they were using to terminate other officers wasn't working when it came to my situation, they added a disciplinary violation on my base file. Headquarters tried using discipline as a reason to fire me from the state service. The impact that a disciplinary violation does to officers is that it plays against them when it's time for them to get another job, apply for another position within the agency, etc. Now a reasonable person would start to wonder, what type of department focuses on destroying people's future? I will go a long way to explain to you all the level of inhumane treatment that exists at the DPSCS. On March 11, 2019, both CDF Wardens Rebecca and Pamela ganged up in an attempt to fire me from the state service by setting up a false employee disciplinary mitigation conference at CDF.

These two women accused me of refusing to attend the medical evaluation appointment that they made without my knowledge. Warden Rebecca and Miss Pamela alleged that they sent me an e-mail, called me on the phone, and sent a letter to my house. In reality, there was no such thing because my e-mail, phone number, or house address was the same as the one they provided in my information. When they found out that they had the wrong information, both of them still countered their mistake against me.

For the sake of peace, on April 25, 2019, I underwent another medical evaluation at Pivot Occupational Health for fitness for duty since I was accused and framed up again for being unfit and mentally imbalanced. The state medical director Doctor Ghansham was the person I saw that day at the appointment. Doctor Ghansham compelled me into signing a no-patient-and-doctor-relationship document. I got the most shocking information about my life from Doctor Ghansham. The state doctor said this to me: "Your agency documented that you threatened a DPSCS official and that individual feels unsafe around you. This incident took place somewhere in October 2018. Also, your agency wants me to send you to another psychological evaluation for mental illness." I informed the state doctor that all allegations from the agency were false information; however, it is as though that DPSCS has instructed Doctor Ghansham on what to write on the evaluation. As a result, Doctor Ghansham concluded his initial workability evaluation of me based on the previous year's culturally biased IQ exam that placed me on a fifth-grade level of reasoning, accused me of lacking social skills, together with the medical classification of me being disabled. Notably, I gave the state medical doctor my primary care doctor's evaluation and my medical history for him to see that I'm being accused wrongfully of having a mental illness and being unfit for duty. Despite the medical evidence that I provided for the state medical director, he still went ahead and supported DPSCS, knowing full well that I was innocent. Doctor Ghansham's initial summary and recommendations he made before referring me to undergo another independent psychological evaluation (IPE) was as follows: "Based on the medical records reviewed, history provided by Miss Margaret Rose, and on physical examination today, it's my opinion that Miss Margaret Rose is unable to safely, consistently, and reliably perform her essential job duties with or without reasonable accommodations at this time."

The state doctor undermined the medical report for work evaluation from my primary care doctor, who was more familiar with my health and my medical history, which vindicated me from being physical or mental ill, which the DPSCS had accused me of and is still accusing me of. In my primary care doctor's work evaluation report, she stated, "Patient can return to work with no restriction." The DPSCS headquarters made up lies about me to their doctor just so I will get terminated from the state service for medical reasons. This drove me to see Mister Thomas, the deputy commissioner, at the O'Brien House. When I got there, Mister Thomas was having a meeting, so I left without seeing him to explain the reason for my visit. On April 26, 2019, I received a letter from DPSCS banning me from entering O'Brien House and all the correctional facilities.

After Warden Rebecca left CDF, Warden Matthew became the new warden of CDF. Miss Pamela ordered the new CDF warden to start using my leave to pay me while I was supposed to still be on paid administrative leave. DPSCS headquarters and Miss Pamela continued interfering with my paychecks and personal leave hours. This new development that Miss Pamela came up with, which was against the department policy, resulted in my receiving 67.8 hours rather than 80 hours. It equally affected my paycheck and, thus, the paying off my bills. When I got the information from the new warden of CDF that the leave hours that I worked so hard to earn were being used, I requested to know the reason. He told me that Miss Pamela gave him a direct order. I reached out to Miss Pamela to know why such orders were given to the warden, she told me this: "Well, Miss Margaret Rose, the state medical doctor said that we shouldn't give you any reasonable accommodation now or in the unforeseen future. So you are on your own." After Miss Pamela finished with her statement, I asked her a few questions, but I never got an answer. My questions were as follows: How come DPSCS headquarters is using my leave hours but am still supposed to be on administrative leave with pay, and on top of that, I'm yet to go for the psychological evaluation that was forced on me by the department? How come the state doctor concluded on my first visit that I was unfit for duty without me going for the psychological evaluation first, without the psychological results coming out, or me coming for final workability evaluation? Why would the state doctor write that I was unfit for duty based on the last year IQ exam that was biased and that I countered against? Why was I banned from entering all the prison facilities? Why would a state doctor, Doctor Ghansham, undermine my primary care doctor's medical reports? Finally, why didn't Doctor Ghansham provide his medical report rather than basing his findings on another doctor's errors?

On May 3, 2019, I went for the psychological evaluation for workability. The evaluation was conducted by Dr. Emma, a licensed psychologist. In the psychological report and recommendation, she stated the following:

> *Brief mental status examination result*: Miss Margaret Rose presented with an agitated affect and depressed mood. She tried to force congeniality and cooperate with procedures; her mood was labile. She spoke fluently in English and expressed her thoughts clearly in normal voice prosody. Her memory appeared to be functional for recent and long-term events. Judgment and reasoning were fair. No indications or reports of any hallucinations, delusions, or other psychotic processes.

House-Tree-Person Projective Drawing: Miss Margaret Rose's drawings suggest she is suspicious and guarded in her approach to environmental interactions. Her trust and belief in the goodwill of others appeared to be compromised, which could be due to the incidents she has experienced in her job.

Beck Depression Inventory (second edition): Miss Margaret Rose's responses yielded a score of 0, which suggests she is not experiencing any symptom of depression. However, it appears that she attempted to give socially acceptable answers to avoid any negative connotations. Drawing strongly suggests depressive symptomology with underlying feelings of powerlessness and helplessness.

Beck Anxiety Inventory: Miss Margaret Rose's response yielded a score of 0. The BAI measures the anxiety level by asking examinees to rate the intensity of thoughts and feelings associated with anxiety.

State-Trait Anger Expression Inventory (second edition): Measuring and assessing an individual's overall social, emotional, and personality adjustment. Miss Margaret Rose's responses reflected positive thoughts about herself and her family. She has an optimistic outlook on life and high aspiration for achievement. She believes in respecting the rights of others. She worries about how others perceive her, and this is contributing to severe distress and depression for her. She has internalized emotional trauma due to her perceptions of bullying and harassment from some of her coworkers. Her personality structure, overall, appears to be reasonably well-adjusted but is impacted at present by her job-related stress and worries. Currently, she is troubled by persecutory thoughts that she is mistreated on her job.

Rotter Incomplete Sentences Blank: STAXI-2 assesses how individuals experience, expresses, and controls anger feelings. Miss Margaret Rose's response was within the average range for state anger, trait anger, and anger expression. Her response was slightly elevated for anger control. She strives to avoid experiencing anger, feelings; but when she does feel angry, she tends to suppress her feelings and exert efforts to control any anger expression. She is more prone to internalizing her feelings, which is effective to avoid any maladaptive expressions of anger, but the tendencies to internalize anger and stress subsequently yield to depression and other mood disturbances. She could benefit from psychotherapy to aid her in coping with the stressor and reduce risks of escalating depression.

Minnesota Multiphasic Personality Inventory (second edition) Restructured Form: Miss Margaret Rose MMPI-2 -RF response suggests she did not overreport thoughts or feelings, but she might have underreported symptoms. Her answers did not show emotion, thought, behavioral, or personality dysfunction. She is experiencing some mistrust and feelings of persecution about the job situation.

Most importantly, Dr. Emma's medical summary indicated,

Personality structure is intact and reasonably well adjusted. She shows capacity for empathy, concern for others, respect for the rights of others, close family ties, and positive outlook on life overall. Her current functioning is impacted by job-related stress and worry. She internalized emotional trauma that impacts her moods and reactions to stressors. Based on this evaluation, Miss Margaret Rose is not psychologically able to perform the essential duties of her position as yet; she has not sufficiently resolved her emotional distress feelings of persecution and internalized trauma. She needs to remain on leave while she initiates counseling. She needs a therapeutic venue to process and resolve her feelings about her work situation before she resumes her duties. When she shows therapeutic progress in emotional resolution and the ability to utilize effective strategies to manage stressors, she should be considered for a transfer to a different location. Her mental health and, subsequently, her job performance will be compromised if she returns to the same work setting with exposure to recurring stressors.

In like manner, my diagnostic impressions illustrated that I have "F43-21: Adjustment disorder with depressed mood. And F43-8: Other specified trauma-and-stressor-related disorder (work-related stress)." Meanwhile, the recommendations were as follows:

It is recommended that Miss Margaret Rose remains on leave while she initiates psychotherapy and counseling. As she shows progress, she should be considered for return to work at a different location. Psychotherapy is recommended for depression, stress, and mood liability and to resolve feelings about her job situation. Miss Margaret Rose should participate in a weekly therapy session initially until she shows progress in resolving her emotional distress. A psychiatric evaluation is recommended for further assessment of symptoms and aid in determining if medication is appropriate.

Nevertheless, on May 23, 2019, I went back to the state medical doctor for workability follow-up. The psychological results weren't available. So, on May 30, 2019, I received a copy of the final workability evaluation from Miss Pamela. Doctor Ghansham used this method during his last evaluation, thinking that I wasn't going to pay attention to them. First, Doctor Ghansham kept restating last year's false medical report from another doctor and relied solely on another doctor's incorrect findings. Doctor Ghansham went back on the reason why DPSCS sent me to workability evaluation. Based on his belief, he stated, "Syncopal episodes." Again, that was a lie. Doctor Ghansham repeated some of the psychologist's findings by saying, "I also referred Miss Margaret Rose for an IPE. Dr. Emma performed an IPE on May 14, 2019. She determined that based on this evaluation, Miss Margaret Rose is not psychologically able to perform the essential duties of her position. As yet, she has not sufficiently resolved her emotional distress, feeling of persecution, and internalized trauma. She needs to remain on leave while she initiates counseling."

Please be advised that the state medical director, Doctor Ghansham, intentionally withheld the most significant part of this psychological evaluation. The state doctor failed to mention the following part of Dr. P. Emma's psychological report: "She needs a therapeutic venue to process and resolve her feelings about her work situation before she resumes her duties. When she shows therapeutic progress in emotional resolution and the ability to utilize effective strategies to manage stressors, she should be considered for a transfer to a different location. Her performance will be compromised if she returns to the same work setting with exposure to recurring stressors."

Then again, Doctor Ghansham's IPE appointment date was wrong. I went to the psychological evaluation on May 3, 2019, not May 14, 2019, as the state doctor wrote. State medical doctor failed to disclose that I suffered from other specified trauma-and-stressor-related disorder (work-related stress). He purposely excluded all the other psychological evaluation reports that were conducted by Dr. Emma. Nonetheless, all he did was to base his findings on a 2018 false medical IQ exam, making it look like something was medically wrong with me. But in reality, I'm medically fine.

This is the method both the state medical doctors and DPSCS uses to terminate correctional officers. Furthermore, the state medical director, Doctor Ghansham, concluded his medical summary by repeating the following: "Based on the medical records reviewed, history provided by Miss Margaret Rose, and on physical examination today, it is my opinion that Miss Margaret Rose is unable to safely, consistently, and reliably perform her essential job duties with or without reasonable accommodations in the near or foreseeable future. It is, therefore, my recommendation that the agency take the appropriate administrative actions concerning her employment status as a correctional officer II."

I will take a minute to explain what just happened here and the game DPSCS and the state doctor, Doctor Ghansham, were trying to play on my intelligence; but before that, did anyone recognize where this statement was made before? Okay, check this out. The above statement was made by Doctor Ghansham on April 25, 2019, during my first medical workability evaluation visit with him. He stated, "Based on the medical records reviewed, history provided by Miss Margaret Rose, and physical examination today, it is my opinion that Miss Margaret Rose is unable to safely, consistently, and reliably perform her essential job duties with or without reasonable accommodations at this time." This was before I went for the psychological evaluation. Again, after the psychological result came out, he repeated the same thing on his final evaluation after reading the full psych report. It goes without saying that the false medical report that the state medical director provided that got me terminated from state service was influenced by the bribe he collected from DPSCS, just like the rest of the other state medical directors. Doctor Ghansham's false medical report that got me unlawfully terminated from state service is a clear light that reflects the corrupt system of the Department of Corruption—sorry, I mean, Corrections. Equally, it's an evidence that showed Doctor Ghansham's biased mind-set toward me, which was a result of the money he took from DPSCS to alter my medical report and the fact that his mind has already been poisoned with the false information that came from the headquarters. DPSCS headquarters insinuated that I threatened one of the officials before I met him. Doctor Ghansham read the psychological report and saw that I needed psychotherapy treatment because of the working conditions I was subjected to starting from 2015 until 2019, and he intentionally failed to disclose the full details, along with the negative impact, of this untreated depression mood and stress would cause me. Despite the danger that untreated depression would cause, Doctor Ghansham still went ahead and recommended the following after he was paid to produce a false medical result: "Agency take the appropriate administrative actions concerning her employment status as a correctional officer II." Doctor Ghansham's actions and behavior were unethical. He violated the oath of his medical practice, which was to save lives rather than to destroy life. Finally, the state doctor's negligence to disclose the full medical results of the psychologist not only violated his medical oath, he likewise allowed himself to be used by DPSCS headquarters. Also, he jeopardized my health as the depressed mood I was experiencing became more intense and painful.

These were the other areas that Doctor Ghansham got caught on his lies. For example, he said, "Miss Margaret Rose requested transfer supervisors transferred her to a position where she performed data analysis." The truth is that I got a job to work as a project manager and statistics data analyst for the DPSCS medical unit. Also, DPSCS medical department was looking for a correctional officer who is educated enough to handle the position and its responsibilities. I, on the other hand, was more than capable of doing the job, so I went for the interview. I was helped by the former warden of CDF, who told the man that hired me the type of person I was and my work ethics. The warden helped me out because she knew that somebody from headquarters would go and poison the mind of the medical chief who was trying to hire me.

Again, Doctor Ghansham lied in his statement when he said, "Miss Margaret Rose was instructed to return to CDF on January 11, 2019. She stated she told her supervisors the same day she reportedly threatened agency official." However, the correct thing that happened was that on January 11, 2019, while I was working at JI Building in the morning of the said date, Major Angela came and ordered me back to the CDF. When I asked her why, she told me, "I'm giving you a direct order." Major Angela took the office key from me, and I went back to the CDF. When I got to CDF, I told the new warden, Warden Rebecca, that I can't work in CDF because of the detainees knowing my personal information including the type of handgun I store in the master control. I informed Warden Rebecca that on October 21, 2018, I wrote a matter of record for transfer. I went to report the issue to Deputy Commissioner Thomas, but he was busy. When I returned to CDF, I was asked to write a matter of record by Warden Rebecca. After the writing, Warden Rebecca placed me on administrative leave. The state medical doctor lied about the reason why I got sent to work evaluation in 2018. He stated, "Stress-related to syncopal episodes." Nevertheless, I was referred for a workability evaluation because the former warden at MRDCC and the BCCC officers and supervisors framed me up into making the headquarters believe that I was crazy just so I would get terminated from state service. Sadly, Doctor Ghansham referring me to psychological evaluation was based on the lies that DPSCS made up. State medical director passed a life-ending and a career-killing judgment on me based on his opinions rather than on medical facts. His medical opinion came as a result of him being paid off by the department to use the approach of illegally terminating officers through medical results. In my case, state medical director's physical examination countered against my primary care doctor's physical examination.

After the state medical director's false report, the department started forcing me to believe that I was medically disabled and couldn't work. I filed a complaint against the state medical director (state doctor) to the Maryland Board of Physicians.

However, two weeks later, I received a mail from the Maryland Board of Physicians intake manager Marilyn informing me that my complaint didn't fall under the forty-three grounds jurisdiction of the board. During my first complaint, I included all the evidence necessary that will help the Maryland Board of Physicians see that there was medical misconduct. Again, I was not all that surprised when I got that letter from the intake manager. In all honesty, I wasn't expecting much. I mean come on. How can it be possible for me to get justice knowing that the person I was reporting of medical misconduct was working under the same state of Maryland? State of Maryland Board of Physicians plus the state medical director plus DPSCS is equal to community cover-up. There was no way I could win that war. Not minding the outcome, I still tried. The main reason why I went to file a complaint to the Board of Physicians and handed them all the documentation was for me to have paperwork on those persons I have reported that were involved on DPSCS's ongoing victimization and the actions that they took to resolve the case. Just like they say, "It's better to have something and not need it, than need something but doesn't have it. Saving for the rainy day."

Without letting the first returned letter from Maryland Board of Physicians to deter me, I went back and sent in a second complaint, detailing the role Doctor Ghansham played in getting me fired. I also gave the board of physicians a copy of the termination letter just for them to see that I was telling the truth. Again, the same intake manager Marilyn sent me another letter stating the following: "Your complaint doesn't fall in the forty-three grounds jurisdiction of the board." Up until today, I still don't understand why a fake doctor and a false medical result didn't fall under the forty-three grounds. The intake manager didn't think it right to explain to me why my complaint didn't fall under forty-three grounds. The intake manager didn't even explain to me what forty-three grounds are.

Here is the Maryland Board of Physician Complaint Form:

DEPARTMENT OF HEALTH AND MENTAL HYGIENE
MARYLAND BOARD OF PHYSICIANS
4201 PATTERSON AVE.BALTIMORE, MD 21215
Phone (410)7644777FAX (410)3581298 TDD FOR DISABLED
MD Relay Service
18007352258
COMPLAINT FORM

Please complete this form and return to:
   Maryland Board of Physicians
   INTAKE UNIT
   4201 Patterson Avenue
   Baltimore, MD 21215

If you have any questions, please call 4107642480 or 18004926836 ext.#
2480.

1. IDENTIFY THE TYPE OF HEALTH PROVIDER:

X Physician	_____Psychiatrist Assistant
_____Radiographer	_____Physician Assistant
_____Nuclear Medical Technologist	_____Respiratory Care Practitioner
_____Radiation Therapist	_____Radiologist Assistant
_____Polysomnographic Technologist	_____Athletic Trainer
_____Naturopathic Doctor	_____Perfusionist

2. IDENTIFY THE HEALTH PROVIDER:

Full Name: Doctor Ghansham
Office Address: 6785 Business Parkway Ste 1&2 (Street)
Elkridge Maryland 21075

3. PATIENT'S NAME:

Full Name: Margaret Rose
Office Telephone: N/A

4. IDENTITY OF COMPLAINANT: The Board cannot guarantee anonymity. Information in the complaint may be shared with the practitioner/licensee. If you wish to remain anonymous, do not include information on the complaint form, envelope, e-mail or other materials that may reveal your identity.

If the person making the complaint is not the patient, please provide the following information:
Full Name: Margaret Rose
Office Telephone: N/A

5. DATE PATIENT WAS TREATED: 04/25/2019 and 05/23/2019

6. THE PHARMACY USED BY THE PATIENT: N/A

7. RELATIONSHIP OF COMPLAINANT TO PATIENT:

| _____ Patient | _____ Spouse |
| _____ Relative | ____X__ No relation |

8. WHAT, IF ANY, ARE YOUR PROFESSIONAL OR PERSONAL RELATIONSHIPS WITH THE HEALTH PROVIDER?

The provider is the Department of Public Safety and Correctional Services state medical director, while I, on the other hand, am a correctional officer II from the same department.

9. STATE NAMES, ADDRESSES, AND TELEPHONE NUMBERS OF ALL PERSONS WHO HAVE KNOWLEDGE OF YOUR COMPLAINT, INCLUDING ANY OTHER HEALTH PROVIDERS.

Noah, Deputy Secretary of Operations for the Department of Public Safety and Correctional Services, and Baltimore City Congressman Ethan.

The Maryland Board of Physicians (MBP) supports the Americans with Disabilities Act and will provide this complaint packet in an alternative format to facilitate effective communication with sensory impaired individuals. (For example, Braille, large print, audio tape.) If you need such accommodation, please notify the MBP ADA designee, Yemisi Koya, at 4107644777; Toll-free Number, 18004926836, or use the Maryland Relay Services TT/Voice number, 18007352258.If you have a complaint concerning the MBP's compliance with the ADA, please contact Ms. Koya.

10. NATURE OF COMPLAINT: PLEASE DESCRIBE, WITH AS MUCH DETAIL AS POSSIBLE, WHAT EVENT OR EVENTS LED TO THE FILING OF THIS COMPLAINT. INCLUDE THE DATES AND REASON FOR SEEING THE HEALTH PROVIDER IN YOUR DESCRIPTION.

State Medical Director Ghansham Medical Misconduct

My name is Margaret Rose. I turned in a medical complaint against the state medical director, Doctor Ghansham; but an intake manager, Marilyn, told me that my complaint doesn't fall in the 43 grounds jurisdiction of the board. However, I don't understand why my complaint didn't fall under 43 grounds. Doctor Ghansham false medical report is about to cost me my job and destroy my life, and on top of that, I have $60,000 worth of student loan to pay back. I will soon lose my medical insurance and become homeless all because of Doctor Ghansham false medical report. My question to the intake manager, Marilyn, is, should I wait and watch my life get destroyed by a medical doctor who took an oath to protect life and is now about to destroy the life that I have worked so hard to build for myself in America? Nevertheless, I will go back to explain in detail how Doctor Ghansham is about to destroy my life by his false medical report: Warden Rebecca sent me on another administrative leave with full pay on January 11, 2019, pending my transfer to the headquarters. On April 22, 2019, I received another letter for a medical work evaluation appointment. On April 26, 2019, I went to Pivot Occupational Health, and Doctor Ghansham saw me. The state doctor told me that the DPSCS said that I threatened a coworker in October 2018, but later changed it to January before I went on administrative leave, but all that was a made-up lies just for them to use a an avenue to fire me. And because of that, they sent me to Pivot Occupational Health. DPSCS headquarters lied again to get me fired from state services. After the state doctor finished hearing my side of the story about the ongoing victimization from the DPSCS, alongside with reviewing my medical history that my primary care doctor gave me as evidence to show that I'm okay to return to work, Doctor Ghansham referred me to a psychological evaluation. Doctor Ghansham informed me that my agency, DPSCS, requested for him to send me to IPE. The state doctor wrote in his summary, saying, "Stay in current position, full report to follow." On May 3, 2019, I went to the psychological evaluation that was located on 8181 Professional Place Ste. 200 Hyestville, MD 20785. Doctor Ghansham went further into making this medically biased decision after looking at last year's false medical report that was again based on an IQ exam that was culturally biased. He stated, "Based on the medical records reviewed, history provided by Miss Margaret Rose and on physical examination today, it is my opinion that Miss Margaret Rose is unable to safely, consistently, and reliably perform her essential job duties with or without reasonable accommodations at this time." State medical director passed a life-ending and a career-killing judgment on me based on his opinions rather than medical facts. His medical opinion resulted in DPSCS taking me off administrative leave and they started using my leave. State medical director's physical examination countered against my primary care doctor's physical exam. Note that I have been with my primary care doctor for so many years, and she knows my health more than anyone else.

After my psychological evaluation on May 3, 2019, Dr. Emma's psychological reports are as follows:

Methods used for psychological evaluations

Tests and measures administered.

Clinical interview with Miss Margaret Rose

Brief mental status examination

House, Tree, and Person projective drawing

Beck depression inventory second edition

Beck anxiety inventory

State-trait anger expression inventory second edition

Rotter incomplete sentences blank

Minnesota Multiphasic Personality Inventory (2nd edition, restructured)

Brief Mental Status Examination result: Miss Margaret Rose presented with an agitated affect and depressed mood. She tried to force congeniality and cooperate with procedures; her mood was labile. She spoke fluently in English and expressed her thoughts clearly in normal voice prosody. Her memory appeared to be functional for recent and long-term events. Judgment and reasoning were fair. No indications or reports of any hallucinations, delusions, or other psychotic processes.

House-Tree-Person Projective Drawing: Miss Margaret Rose drawings suggest she is suspicious and guarded in her approach to environmental interactions. Her trust and belief in the goodwill of others appeared to be compromised, which could be due to the incidents she has experienced in her job.

Beck Depression Inventory, second edition: Miss Margaret Rose's responses yielded a score of 0, which suggests she is not experiencing any symptom of depression. However, it appears that she attempted to give socially acceptable answers to avoid any negative connotations. Drawing strongly suggests depressive symptomology with underlying feelings of powerlessness and helplessness.

Beck Anxiety Inventory: Miss Margaret Rose's response yielded a score of 0. The BAI measures anxiety level by asking examinees to rate the intensity of thoughts and feelings associated with anxiety.

State-Trait Anger Expression Inventory, second edition: Measuring and assessing an individual's overall social, emotional, and personality adjustment. Miss Margaret Rose's responses reflected positive thoughts about herself and her family. She has an optimistic outlook on life and high aspiration for achievement. She believes in respecting the rights of others. She worries about how others perceive her, and this is contributing to severe distress and depression for her. She has internalized emotional trauma due to her perceptions of bullying and harassment from some of her co-workers. Her personality structure overall appears to be reasonably well-adjusted but is impacted at present by her job-related stress and worries. Currently, she is troubled with persecutory thoughts that she is treated unfairly on her job.

Rotter Incomplete Sentences Blank: STAXI-2 assesses how individuals experience, express, and control anger feelings. Miss Margaret Rose's response was within the average range for state anger, trait anger, and anger expression. Her response was slightly elevated for anger control. She strives to avoid experiencing anger feelings, but when she does feel angry, she tends to suppress her feelings and exert efforts to control any anger expression. She is more prone to internalizing her feelings, which is effective to avoid any maladaptive expressions of anger, but tendencies to internalize anger and stress subsequently yield to depression and other mood disturbances. She could benefit from psychotherapy to aid her in coping with the stressor and reduce risks of escalating depression.

Minnesota Multiphasic Personality Inventory, 2nd edition, restructured form: Miss Margaret Rose's MMPI-2 -RF response suggests she did not overreport thoughts or feelings, but she might have underreported symptoms. Her answers did not show emotional, thought, behavioral, or personality dysfunction. She is experiencing some mistrust and feelings of persecution in relation to the job situation.

Summary and conclusions: Personality structure is intact and reasonably well adjusted. She shows capacity for empathy concern for others, respect for the rights of others, close family ties, and positive outlook on life overall. Her current functioning is impacted by job-related stress and worry. She internalized emotional trauma that impacts her moods and reactions to stressors. Based on this evaluation, Miss Margaret Rose is not psychologically able to perform the essential duties of her position as yet; she has not sufficiently resolved her emotional distress feelings of persecution and internalized trauma. She needs to remain on leave while she initiates counseling. She needs a therapeutic venue to process and resolve her feelings about her work situation before she resumes her duties. When she shows therapeutic progress in emotional resolution and ability to utilize effective strategies to manage stressors, she should be considered for a transfer to a different location. Her mental health and subsequently, her job performance will be compromised if she returns to the same work setting with exposure to recurring stressors.

Diagnostic impressions:

F43-21: Adjustment disorder with depressed mood.

F43-8: Other specified trauma-and stressor-related disorder (work-related stress).

Recommendations:

It is recommended that Miss Margaret Rose remain on leave while she initiates psychotherapy and counseling. As she shows progress, she should be considered for return to work at a different location.

Psychotherapy is recommended for depression, stress, and mood liability and to resolve feelings about her job situation. Miss Margaret Rose should participate in a weekly therapy session initially until she shows progress in resolving her emotional distress.

A psychiatric evaluation is recommended for further assessment of symptoms and aid in determining if medication is appropriate.

Consultation with her treatment providers is recommended to assess progress and determine when she should return to work.

ITEM 10. NATURE OF COMPLAINT, CONTINUED:

On May 23, 2019, I went back to the state doctor, and on May 30, 2019, the final medical workability result came out. The state medical doctor wrote on his report that DPSCS should not give me any reasonable medical accommodation now or in the nearby future. And based on his opinion, I should be fired from state service. Doctor Ghansham undermined the psychological and medical report for me to start treatment and get my life back; and he went on creating more pain, stress, and depression for me by lying on my medical report so that I can get fired and lose all that I have ever worked for here in America. Doctor Ghansham's final reports stated the following:

Doctor Ghansham kept restating last year another doctor's false medical report that he relayed solely on another doctor's incorrect findings. Doctor Ghansham went back on previous year reason of why DPSCS sent me to workability evaluation, which he stated, "syncopal episodes." Again, that was a lie. Doctor Ghansham noted the following to represent Dr. Patricial Emma's findings: "I also referred Miss Margaret Rose for an IPE. Dr. Patricial Emma performed an IPE on May 14, 2019. She determined that based on this evaluation, Miss Margaret Rose is not psychologically able to perform the essential duties of her position. As yet, she has not sufficiently resolved her emotional distress, feeling of persecution, and internalized trauma. She needs to remain on leave while she initiates counseling." Please be advised that the state medical director, Doctor Ghansham, intentionally withheld the most significant part of this psychological evaluation. The state doctor failed to mention these following parts of Dr. Emma's report: "She needs a therapeutic venue to process and resolve her feelings about her work situation before she resumes her duties. When she shows therapeutic progress in emotional resolution and ability to utilize effective strategies to manage stressors, she should be considered for a transfer to a different location. Her performance will be compromised if she returns to the same work setting with exposure to recurring stressors." State medical doctor failed to disclose that I suffered from other specified trauma- and stressor-related disorder (work-related stress). He negligently didn't include all the other psychological evaluation reports that were conducted by Dr. Emma. Nonetheless, all he did was to base his findings on 2018 false medical report to make me look bad and loss my job rather than helping me to get the medical help that I need as a doctor. Furthermore, state medical director Ghansham concluded his medical summary by stating the following: "Based on the medical records reviewed, history provided by Miss Margaret Rose, and on physical examination today, it is my opinion that Miss Margaret Rose is unable to safely, consistently, and reliably perform her essential job duties with or without reasonable accommodations in the near or foreseeable future. It is, therefore, my recommendation that the agency takes the appropriate administrative actions concerning her employment status as a correctional officer II." Please, vital information to notice in the state doctor's final summary: on April 25, 2019, Doctor Ghansham stated the following: "Based on the medical records reviewed, history provided by Miss Margaret Rose, and physical examination today, it is my opinion that Miss Margaret Rose is unable to safely, consistently, and reliably perform her essential job duties with or without reasonable accommodations at this time." So, on May 23, 2019, the state doctor made the same statement concerning my job. It is a clear indication that DPSCS bribed the state doctor to produce a bias medical report that headquarters, or should I say Miss Pamela, manager of employee relation unit, will use to fire me from state service. Equally, this is an evidence to show that the state doctor, Doctor Ghansham, already had a biased mind toward me prior before meeting me in his office for the first time and before sending me to the psychological evaluation. Without speculating, Doctor Ghansham read the psychological report and saw that I needed a medical help based on the conditions in which I was subjected to at work since 2015 to date, and he intentionally failed to disclose it. However, the state doctor still went ahead and recommended this to DPSCS based on the misleading medical report he made up: "Agency take the appropriate administrative actions concerning her employment status as a correctional officer II." Doctor Ghansham actions and behaviors are medically unethical. He violated the oath of his medical practice, which is to save lives, not destroy life. Finally, the state doctor's negligence to make a full medical report has not only caused me more depression but have also created an endless mental, physical, and employment pains and worries. Because of the state medical doctor's false medical report, on June 4, 2019, DPSCS placed my picture and name all over Maryland jails like a common criminal. On June 5, 2019, I got a letter from DPSCS asking me to resign from the state service or get fired as a correctional officer. Also, because of Doctor Ghansham medical report, on June 20, 2019, DPCS requested for me to resign again, they are forcing me to believe that I have medical issues that I don't have. Doctor Ghansham's false medical report is about to cost me my job, career, and life. I need justice. I have already sent in all the documents to the intake department on June 12, 2019. Please help me. Doctors took an oath to save lives, not to destroy them.

11. IF THE DIAGNOSIS AND TREATMENT THAT WAS RENDERED, WHICH IS THE SUBJECT OF THIS COMPLAINT, WAS PAID BY THIRD PARTY INSURER, IDENTIFY INSURER AND PATIENT'S INSURANCE IDENTIFICATION NUMBER.

Insurance Identification Number: N/A
Insurance Company Name: N/A
Insurance Company Address: N/A

12. LIST THE IDENTITY OF ANY PERSONS TO WHOM YOU HAVE MADE A SIMILAR COMPLAINT, INDICATE WHEN THE COMPLAINT WAS MADE.

First this is the second time the DPSCS state medical doctor is lying on my medical report. Also, I have heard a lot of correctional officers saying that the state doctors lied on their medical report, but I know that many of them are afraid to speak up because they are afraid of getting fired from state service or even get killed.

13. ATTACH COPIES OF ANY REPORTS, BILLS, INVOICES, DOCUMENTS, OR STUDIES SUPPORTING OR RELATING TO YOUR CLAIM.

Copies of Supporting Documents Attached: Yes

14. I HEREBY ATTEST THAT THE FOREGOING INFORMATION IS TRUE TO THE BEST OF MY KNOWLEDGE AND BELIEF, AND THAT I AM COMPETENT TO MAKE THESE STATEMENTS.

June 21, 2019   Margaret Rose
_____   _____
Date of Complaint   Signature of Complainant

15. RELEASE OF MEDICAL RECORDS

I hereby consent to the release to the Maryland Board of Physicians, or its designated investigating body, of medical reports and records related to this occurrence from any hospital, related institution, or physician, including the physician who is the subject of this complaint.

If the Maryland Board of Physicians determines that this complaint is a fee dispute, I consent to sending this complaint to the Consumer Protection Division of the Attorney General's office for mediation.

Yes.

If block is not checked, this complaint will be dismissed if the Board finds no probable violation of the Maryland Medical Practice Act.

16. RELEASE OF ADDITIONAL INFORMATION

I hereby consent to the release of any reports, responses, or any other material that the Maryland Board of Physicians deems necessary from any health care provider who provided treatment to me whether or not this health care provider is mentioned in any part of this complaint.

June 10, 2019   Margaret Rose
_____   _____

Date of Complaint   Signature of Complainant

08/29/13, Revised 10/24/14, 03/20/15, 04/28/16

Before I proceed further, I will like to shed light on this crucial aspect of the Department of Corrections. Inside the DPSCS, there are two main types of facilities. These are the Department of Corrections (DOC) and the Department of Pretrial Detention and Services Division (DPDS). Department of Corrections is where inmates who are serving their prison terms are kept. On the other hand, Pretrial Detention is where detainees who are waiting for their trials and have not yet been sentenced are kept. Now that these two things have been clarified, I will go back to my initial thought. On June 4, 2019, after DPSCS state medical doctor conspired with the headquarters to manipulate a false medical result against me, DPSCS displayed my picture in all Baltimore downtown pretrials facilities, offices, and other parts of DOC jails as well. DPSCS posted my pictures in a written memo that stated the following:

> Banned employee—Officer Margaret Rose, sent on behalf of Deputy Commissioner Thomas, Esq. Effective immediately, Officer Margaret Rose, who is assigned to the Chesapeake Detention Center (CDF), is at this moment banned from all Division of Pretrial Detention and Services facilities: to include MRDCC and JI entry and exit post. This memo shall be posted on all DPDS entry and exit post of DPDS institutions. Please note: This officer wears various hairstyles and hair colors (blond). If Officer Margaret Rose attempts to enter any DPDS institution, please immediately contact the supervisor.

This post went viral in all the DPSCS jails. Officers, inmates, detainees, inmates/detainees' visitors, officers from other prisons, visitors from all parts of America who came to visit their family inside the DPSCS facilities saw this dehumanizing picture of me with the lies DPSCS made up. Defamation of character was made on me by the department of corruption that I worked for. DPSCS posted this memo three weeks before I was illegally terminated from the state service. The department framed me up and made me look like a terrorist who is crazy and is an endangerment to the society. They dehumanized and victimized every part of my being. I was set up, and my self-image was destroyed by the DPSCS.

My case alone will give you all a better understanding of the reason why officers are being killed on and off duty. It will show you that all the correctional officers the DPSCS showed on TV as people who committed a crime are all lies. The DPSCS is framing up innocent correctional officers and sending them to jail. Again, innocent DPSCS correctional officers are intentionally sentenced out of spite, hatred, and jealousy from the department. The DPSCS tortured, discriminated, dehumanized, and victimized me from 2015 to 2019. They have tried all they could to frame me up so that I could get locked up. DPSCS has also tried killing me many times but was unsuccessful, so they utilized this method of torturing, hoping that I will take my own life out of depression. The department saw my psychological report, but they tried using it against me by mentally pushing me into killing myself. But today, I stand tall and strong in the name of my Lord Jesus to say, "DPSCS, you all have failed. He that is in me is greater than he that is in you all. I'm made in heaven. I don't walk alone. DPSCS, I don't fight alone. He who fights an innocent person should be cautious because the sins of the father shall visit their children and their six generations to come. The same way you all ganged up against me, paid my kindness with pain, framed me up, victimized me, dehumanized me, tortured me, discriminated against me, made up lies against me, destroyed everything that I have worked for all my life, provided false medical documentation against me, and unlawfully terminated me from state service.

"He who saw me going through this pain from 2015 to 2019, he who was in a position to help during my case but failed to, he who was in DPSCS leadership position that saw what happened to me but failed to exclude himself by doing the right thing. And he who sits one side laughing at me while this case was going on, together with those who provided the idea or the medical reports that were used to victimize me, I place a curse on you all today. Let all you have done onto me be done back onto you all and your generations that are here now and thousands yet to come. As long as I'm serving the living God, the measurement in which you all used and measured for me shall equally be used on you all. Strangers shall take over all your positions and possessions. Your enemies shall gang up and overthrow you all from the positions you all were meant to be in. During the most difficult hours of your lives, there shall never be anybody around to help."

As if this situation that I was in wasn't bad enough, on June 5, 2019, I received a letter from Miss Pamela and other high-ranking individuals in the department, giving me three options and mandating that I must choose one out of the three options. DPSCS headquarters was forcing me to resign, get fired, or request for medical leave without pay. They claimed that I was medically disabled and unfit for duty. Miss Pamela and rest from the headquarters gave me until June 13, 2019, to resign from state service or get terminated. As my life was crumbling, DPSCS made sure that both the leave hours that I acquired and the pay that I was receiving as of that time went down the drain too.

During the last hour of my life when I thought all hope was lost, I also ran out of ideas on what to do. The next thing I did was to go outside of my house and raised my two hands up in the heaven. I cried out to heaven for them to come for my aid. This was my prayer:

"God of justice, God of the innocent, and God of the poor, hear my cry, and let my cry shakes the heaven and anger you. Come because the men of the earth are trying to stop me from serving the Divine purpose in which you have sent me here on earth to do. Show me that you are the living God that I serve. Don't let my enemies laugh at me, rather shame them all. Tell me what to do because I have run out of ideas. God, if this is the way you have meant for me to end up on this earth, then let your will be done. Give me the grace to accept the things that I can't change and the ability to change the things that I can. God, is this the end of the road for me? Angels of God, where are you all? I need heaven's divine intervention. God I'm innocent. Reward me for my good behavior. Tell me what to do. Jesus, are you there? Angels of God, can you all hear me? God, can you see me? Is there anyone home up there? Immaculate Heart of Mary, Mommy, can you hear me? Can you see me? Heaven, please do something. Say something to me."

As I was saying all these things, I was crying. Do you all know what happened after these prayers? Well, let me tell you, people, the full downloads that I received. In less than a second afterward, I was filled with unbelievable abilities. Ideas were running through me like water. I became more fearless. I was being controlled on what to say, who to write, etc. All the actions and words that I wrote to DPSCS was flowing through me. I wasn't the person who was writing the letters and taking those actions. Also, I was instructed to send a letter to a Baltimore City congressman and file a complaint against DPSCS to the Civil Rights Commission. And through this prayer was where I got my writing inspiration. By the way, whoever that said or believed that there is no God, I'm here to confirm and confess to you all that heaven, Jesus, Blessed Virgin Mary, and Archangel Michael are all real; and I have seen them in the dream. So through my prayers during that last hour of my life, when I thought all hope was lost, that was when I gained a new beginning through divine inspiration.

Without throwing people off balance, let me return to what I was saying. The governor of Maryland gave salary increases to all state employees and additional salary increase bonus to all the DPSCS correctional officers. According to this salary increase given by the governor: "In January 2019, all state employees received a 2% salary increase COLA, additional .05% and 3% salary increase. Correctional officers received a 4% salary increase for a total salary increase of 10%. A one-time $500 bonus on April 1, 2019." Governor Hogan approved several incentive programs to improve DPSCS's ability to recruit and retain correctional officers, including a $5,000 recruitment bonus and a $3,000 attendance and retention bonus. DPSCS has seen a decline in both the number of correctional officer retirements and overall employee separations over the past year. In all indications, this salary increase became effective on January 1, 2019; and as of that time, I was still a correctional officer working in JI Building. It was January 11, 2019, when I was sent on administrative leave, so by law, I was entitled to receive both the state employee's salary increase and correctional officer's additional salary increase, which came to a total of 10 percent, alongside with $3,000 attendance and retention bonus and one-time $500 bonus.

In my case, the DPSCS never gave me the $3,000 or the 10 percent salary increase. Also, they still defaulted in paying me the state of Maryland standard salary and the state employee's pay increase the governor gave everybody. After the state employee's salary increase, the standard salary for in the state of Maryland in 2019, which became effective on January 1, 2019, for grade 13, step 4 is $1,650.47, excluding the additional pay increase of state correctional officers. On January 1, 2019, as other state employees and correctional officers were getting their salary increase, I, on the other hand, was still getting below 80 hours. And in addition to lower wages, I got 78.0 hours and was paid $1580.80. I was paid below the standard salary of a correctional officer II in the year 2016 and below the standard salary of a correctional officer II in 2018 and 2019. My payment for January 1, 2019, was made without the state employee's pay increase together with the additional increase for the state correctional officers. From January 15, 2019, to January 29, 2019, salary was paid without the additional salary increase given to the correctional officers. The state employees' standard payment for grade 13, step 4, on the effective date of January 1, 2019, was $1650.47. This salary excluded the additional salary of the correctional officers. Meanwhile, I was paid $1650.40. On April 1, 2019, the standard salary for state employee for grade 13, step 4 was $1658.76, but on April 9, 2019, payment of $1,656.20 was made, which was below the salary of every state employee under my grade and step. Also, I never received the additional salary increase for the officers. Salary of $1658.70 was paid to me without the additional officer's pay increase on April 23, 2019. On June 4, 2019, I received a total of 67.8 hours and a salary of $1406.60.

This was below state of Maryland's salary standard of a correctional officer I. The same thing happened on June 18, 2019. The salary was paid but excluded the additional pay increase of the officers. On August 7, 2019, I received a final payout of $41.91. In addition to all these low wages, throughout my career as a correctional officer, the standard shift differential for my shift, which was three-to-eleven, was $50.00. But I received payments that were less than the $50.00 shift differential starting from 2015 until 2019. For example, on January 19, 2016, I received $45.00. On May 10, 2016, it was $35.00. On May 24, 2016, it was $25.00; and on November 22, 2016, it was $20.23. Furthermore, on January 17, 2017, I had a shift differential of $35.00. On October 10, 2017, I received $0.00 on shift differential with 49.0 hours regular hours, etc. Unfortunately, I encountered overtime payment issues throughout my career as well. Also, after the 10 percent salary increase rate for every correctional officer and other salary increase that was given to the state of Maryland DPSCS correctional officers on July 1, 2019, the standard salary for state of Maryland correctional officer II, under the grade 13, step 4 was $46,326.00. On the contrary, the total salary that I made as a correctional officer II in grade 13, step 4 was $43,246.00 as of July 10, 2019. This is a clear indication that the DPSCS intentionally deprived me the right to receive and earn fair salary wages while working as a correctional officer under their department. Through the Transamerica benefit paperwork I gave DPSCS headquarters to fill out the employer's section, I discovered my annual salary.

Another negative side of my experience working for the DPSCS was that on January 7, 2019, four days before I was sent on administrative leave, I became aware that all the leave hours I had in the agency's time clock plus system has been reduced. Without overly emphasizing my professional work ethics and the attendance about coming to work promptly, I hardly call in sick, but I discovered that the total sick time I had was 16.26 hours and preschool holiday of 88.00 hours. In like manner, the system gave me 48.00 hours of personal leave, annual leave of 190.57 hours, admin leave of 24.40 hours, and absence hours of 0.00 as my overall accumulative hours from 2014 to 2019. DPSCS, out of spite, took all the hours that I accumulated throughout my career as a correctional officer. Sadly, before I got fired, the manager for employee relation informed me that I had zero hours left from the department time clock plus system. That's how I lost all the hours that I invested from the beginning of my career to the end. DPSCS took all my hard-earned hours. They intentionally maneuvered their time clock plus system just because they were in the position.

Consequently, after receiving the threat to resign or get terminated from DPSCS headquarters on June 5, 2019, I decided to go against the grain and break the code of silence. I reached out to the Baltimore City congressman, Ethan, for help on June 10, 2019.

June 5, 2019

Baltimore City Congressman Ethan

Your attention on: The Department of Public Safety and Correctional Service Injustice System.

My name is Margaret Rose. I'm from Nigeria but moved to America when I was young for a better life and opportunity. Also, I have never stopped believing in the American dream of a better life for myself. Then again, knowing that with hard work, determination, focus, and consistency will get me to the American dream motivated me into working endlessly since I came to the United States until today with hope for a better life in America. Mr. Ethan, I'm a correctional officer II, who is currently on her second forced administrative leave pending illegal termination. The DPSCS is trying to rob me the joy of pursuing liberty, life, and happiness that I deserve, all because I'm an immigrant and a nobody.

Nonetheless, I will give you some of the background information about myself, to explain to you how hard I have worked. First, I'm currently doing my master degree program in homeland security and criminal justice with 3.5010 GPA. I obtained a bachelor's in criminal justice with a degree honor, an associate degree in law enforcement and correctional administration, and a certificate on forensic investigation. I'm a DNA collector for the state of Maryland Public Safety, traffic officer, project manager, and statistical data analyst for the DPSCS. I am a high school motivational speaker, alongside with my affiliations as a member of the Society for Collegiate Leadership and Achievement, forensic sciences organizations, and student government club.

Sir, all these my hard work and so many others are about to get destroyed by the DPSCS after June 13, 2019, and I *need your help to assist me in protecting both my life and future here in America from DPSCS.*

Without wasting much of your time, I will lead you step by step as to how all these issues started and the effort that I made to resolve the issues on discrimination, workplace harassment, bullying, abuse of power, ganging up, receiving a death threat, three illegal attempts to fire me from state service, false medical report, etc. Please exercise patience with me because this problem started from 2015 to present. No one wants to help a nobody like me, and all they are trying to do is to destroy the life that I have made for myself here in this country. It all started this way.

I was hired as a correctional officer for DPSCS on December 1, 2014, and got posted at the BCCC in Downtown Baltimore. On Friday, January 30, 2015, I graduated from the academy, and on February 2, 2015, I began working at BCCC with an assigned FTO, Corporal James, on the seven-to-three shift. Notably, on Friday, March 13, 2015, I completed the FTO training and was placed on the three-to-eleven shift. Unfortunately, starting from August 2015 until 2018, I was discriminated against, harassed, and bullied by my fellow correctional officers, namely Corporal Patricia, Corporal Linda, and Corporal Elizabeth. They all worked on the eleven-to-seven shift while I was on the three-to-eleven shift. These officers called me "African bitch" and other dehumanizing names. They told me to go back to Africa.

Like I was taught in the academy, I reported these officers to their supervisors, who are Lieutenant Christine, Lieutenant Richard, Captain Christopher, and Major Brian, but nothing was done about it. Instead, these officers came back with more of their cliques to harass me even more. On May 30, 2017, BCCC ex-inmate assaulted me in the parking lot. The police was called, and DPSCS Internal Investigation Division got notified, but nothing was done about it. DPSCS covered it up. Moving forward, on

Thursday, July 6, 2017, I saw Corporal Maria, who work on the seven-to-three shift but came to the three-to-eleven shift for overtime, flirting with inmate Noah, who slept on B side of the tier, right in front of me while working on the North Wing Lower. Going into detail about Corporal Maria's behavior, she opened her leg, brought her hair down, and was touching herself. The inmate, on the other hand, was standing in between Corporal Maria's legs, holding his private part. Inmate Noah gave Corporal Maria a small white paper when she came back. Inmate Noah stated this to her, "Have you taking care of that for me?" Corporal Maria responded, "Not yet." Corporal Maria also was blowing kisses at the inmate. When Corporal Maria left my post, I called Corporal Ava and told her what I witnessed. Corporal Ava, on the other hand, advised me to write a matter of record, but I refused.

However, I explain to Corporal Ava that Corporal Maria and her friends will come after me. Nevertheless, I was forced to write the matter of record against Corporal Maria by the following supervisors: Lieutenant Charlotte, Captain Donna, and Major Brian. However, just like I anticipated, on Wednesday, July 19, 2017, Corporal Maria and her friends Elizabeth and Ella entered my post in south wing lower. As soon as they left the housing unit, all the inmates started acting up for no reason, but I managed to control the situation. That was the beginning of another bullying and harassment by my fellow correctional officers. Corporal Maria later came back the same day and requested for me to go and rewrite the matter of record I wrote. She stated this to me: "What you saw never happened." The next day I informed Major Brian about Corporal Maria's request. As if that wasn't enough, Corporal Maria, Corporal Margaret, and others in their cliques joined together with the first set of eleven-to-seven-shift officers and continued to harass me, including trying to use inmates to hurt me. Corporal Margaret and Corporal Marie threatened me with a statement. They said to me, "If you didn't rewrite the matter of record that you wrote, we would tell everybody that you are flirting with inmates and we will destroy your name in DOC." I kept reporting these officers to Major Brian and Captain Donna. Neither Major Brian nor Captain Donna did anything to stop them. Lieuteant Michael tried his best, but there were too many American supervisors.

Congressman, it will interest you to know that the DPSCS is highly racist and is discriminatory toward immigrants, especially Nigerian immigrant correctional officers. And I happened to be a victim. The DPSCS practices Africans vs. Americans treatment. Meaning that the Americans will cover up for their fellow Americans and punish immigrants. Sir, do you know that the DPSCS has destroyed a lot of Nigerians correctional officers' life in America. Also, are you aware that you can hardly, or should I say, never see immigrants working in headquarters because DPSCS sees us as nobodies from underdeveloped countries? If you don't believe me, please conduct an investigation and you will be surprised what illegal activities you will discover at the DPSCS.

On July 27, 2017, Thursday, Corporal Margaret came to my post on North Wing Lower and started accusing me of flirting with inmates after Marie and her friend left DPSCS. Another incident that occurred was when Officer Helen came back from the academy and started dating my friend Corporal Liam. When Corporal Liam broke up with her, she told the first and second groups of officers who have been harassing me that I took her boyfriend from her. So these officers teamed up together. Their names are Corporal Elizabeth, Corporal Linda, Corporal Patricia, Corporal Margaret, Corporal Dorothy, Corporal Karen, etc.; and they started bullying me even more. I kept notifying the supervisors. Nothing was done about it, as a these officers are friendly with the supervisors. Sir, please be advised that all *these officers are from the seven-to-three and eleven-to-seven shifts while I worked on the three-to-eleven shift.*

Additionally, Corporal Elizabeth accused me of having sex with Summerville and Major Brian. She extended it by saying that "I want all the male officers at BCCC, including Corporal Takin." This false information went viral in all the DPSCS jails, and as a result, all the female officers in all the jails I got sent to are afraid that I would take their boyfriends from them. Unsurprisingly, the supervisors at the BCCC saw what these officers were doing to me, but none of them tried anything to stop them except Lieutenant Michael. Almost all of them turned a blind eye. On December 19, 2017, Lieutenant Iesha Charlotte and Captain Donna informed me that a death threat had been made on my life. Captain Donna tried forcing me to sign a waiver of the liability for the state of Maryland in the event DPSCS correctional officers finally kill me. Then again, on December 20, 2017, Wednesday, Captain Donna brought back the same paper and asked me to sign it, and I refused because I did fear for my life. When I refused to sign my life away, both the correctional officers who have been harassing, bullying, and discriminating against me, Captain Donna and Captain Ruth, ganged up and increased the abuse and victimization. Captain Donna gave an order to other supervisors for them not to allow me inside the officers' roll call or in the jail. The order Captain Donna placed against me resulted in me eating spoilt food while at work because I was banned from putting my food in the officers' refrigerator.

On the same December 20, 2017, at approximately 11:13 p.m., I sent an e-mail to Assistant Warden Jeffrey of MRDCC. I explained to Assistant Warden Jeffrey about my working condition. On December 23, 2017, I also e-mailed him, again updating him on how bad the harassment is getting and at the same time requesting to be sent to the headquarters for my safety. That requested was turned down. On December 31, 2017, Captain Ruth, who used to be the timekeeper lieutenant, continued harassing me. She told me that I'm unfit to be a correctional officer because I'm too nice and act too feminine. Captain Ruth went further to tell me that I will not work in the master control center because of the way I talk and that I need to change the way I sound and talk before I work in the master control center so that the American correctional officers can understand me. She started making comments about my voice and also my handwriting. Captain Ruth went as far as telling other supervisors, such as Sergeant Olivia, Captain Christopher, and Lieutenant Charlotte, to tell me to change the way I talk and sound. On January 2, 2018, at approximately 10:15 p.m., I sent another letter to MRDCC Assistant Warden Jeffrey; and on the January 3, 2018, he responded to my e-mail.

However, he referred me back to the same supervisors who have discriminated, bullied, and harassed me. I couldn't handle the discrimination, harassment, bullying, and the unfair treatment that I was receiving; and on top of that, Warden Kimberly wasn't willing to assist me. I cried every day at work, wishing that one of these people could do the right thing, but none of them did. The victimization got worse; so on January 12, 2018, I went to the DPSCS EEO office, thinking that they were going to help me. But they never did. On the same day, I called the DPSCS Internal Investigation Division for help. Surprisingly, I was told that their department don't investigate a death threat until after it occurs and, because of that, they can't help me. In addition to this, I was sent to MRDCC on temporarily deployment (TDY). MRDCC is one-minute walking distance from BCCC. On January 13, 2018 I wrote a matter of record to be transferred out because Officer Marie, who I made a wrote-up previously, was an MRDCC officer before she was TDY to BCCC and her friends at MRDCC started bullying me again. On January 23, 2018, while at MRDCC, Captain Michelle started harassing just like the supervisors from BCCC when I was working at 3 CM corridor medical unit. The officers from the seven-to-three and eleven-to-seven shifts, together with the seven-to-three-shift supervisors all ganged up and lied, saying that I was crazy and that I'm causing a problem at BCCC to Warden Kimberly, Assistant Warden Jeffrey, and Security Chief Mark just to cover up. At this time I was eating spoiled food at work because I couldn't use the officers' refrigerator.

Disappointedly, Security Chief Mark told me while I was at MRDCC on January 12, 2018, that it's easy for them to say that I am causing the problem at BCCC than going to fix the actual problem. He advised me to resign and that I don't belong to Correction. He went further to say that I should be in law school, be a paralegal or minister of God. Then again, he added the following: "DOC is a corrupt system, the system is built to be corrupt. You will get hurt or killed if you try to change the system." I have been told that I have to "suck a dick, bend over, or have a connection before I can work in the DPSCS headquarters" and that it's not what I know but whom I know and that the DOC will fire me first before letting a nobody like me to work in the headquarters. Warden Kimberly told me that I will get stabbed by an inmate and that I will never be a case manager. On January 31, 2018, at approximately 1:53 p.m., I sent an e-mail to the secretary of the state, but he didn't respond to my e-mail. On January 31, 2018, I passed out at MRDCC as a result of the victimization and dehumanized treatment. On February 13, 2018, at approximately 2:40 p.m., I went back to BCCC because the officers and supervisors who are victimizing me were all on the seven-to-three and eleven-to-seven shifts. But again, I worked on the three-to-eleven shift, and I got along with all the coworkers on my shift.

The same officers, Captain Ruth and Captain Donna started harassing, discriminating, and bullying me again. Captain Donna and Captain Ruth went back and lied to *the warden again, and I was TDY again to MRDCC. I tried to explain to Warden Kimberly what was going on, but she was busy yelling at me. This is due to the racial war at DPSCS that was and still going on between the natural-born Americans and immigrants. I had another stress attack and passed out the second time at MRDCC on February 15. I left in an ambulance again. When I came back to work on February 20, 2018, Warden Kimberly tried forcing me to resign from state service, and when I refused, she made up lies that I was crazy. The BCCC supervisors, officers, and administrators joined her. They all told the headquarters that I was unfit to be an officer just to cover up what they did to me. I was forced on administrative leave by Warden Kimberly on February 20, 2018. I went to the workability evaluation for mental health status at WorkPro on February 28, 2018. The state doctor, Doctor Robert, findings were as follows: no mental illness and thought processes were logical. He continued with his findings by making the following comments: "Due to issues with work harassment leading to multiple stress reactions and the anxiety about going to work, I have concerns about her mental health status and will refer her for a psychiatric evaluation to evaluate her mental health stability and any potential for workplace violence."*

On March 14, 2018, at approximately noon, I went to the neuropsychological workability evaluation test that was conducted by Doctor Robert. His findings were as follows: "An acute stress reaction as a result of the harassment at work." In addition to this, Doctor Robert's report stated the following: "Rapport was established easily. Miss Margaret Rose communicated with adequate vocabulary and sentence structure, was tested for over 4 hours during which she applied herself without excessive tiring or loss of focus. Also, there was no indication of psychotic thought process, delusional, or hallucinatory thinking. In language tasks, no instances of paraphasia or agnosia were noted; there were no notable signs of perseverative or compulsive thinking or behavior. And there were no notable signs of depressive, anxious, hypomanic or manic behaviors." Doctor Robert equally added in his report that I don't have bipolar nor Beck's depression and anxiety. So mentally I was fine. Surprisingly, Doctor Robert diagnosed me with borderline intellectual functioning, intellectual disabilities (assumed to due to cultural background). His diagnosis came as a result of an IQ exam. He said that my achievement test or failure to follow the test instructions placed me at fifth-grade comprehension levels and that I am the cause of my problem at work. He said a lot of things that weren't true in his report. Headquarters attempted firing me based on a culturally biased IQ exam but were unsuccessful.

On April 19, 2018, I was ordered to write a letter about reasonable accommodation. On April 23, 2018, I passed the case management specialist trainee test. I got placed on the better-qualified category. I was supposed to go for an interview but was intentionally denied the opportunity of it because Warden Kimberly told me that I would never be a case manager. On April 24, 2018, at approximately 2:53 p.m., I saw my full medical report and reacted against the IQ test aspect of it. On May 30, 2018, DPSCS EEO Raju forced me to agree that I have a disability. Based on a biased IQ exam, I refused but he still gave me the paper that said that I have a disability. On the same day, I called Mildred, a lady who works with the secretary of the state office, and explained to her my situation. She said this to me: "We all know that you don't reason like a fifth grader." On May 31, 2018, at approximately 7:48 a.m. I sent an e-mail to Mister Raju, clearly stating myself to him that I didn't and had never had a disability all my life. I started working at the Chesapeake Detention Facility (CDF) on June 6, 2018, and on June 20, I became a CDF officer. Most of the officers at CDF believed that I was crazy, take the boyfriends of female officers, and write officers up. I was still facing the same ongoing discrimination, victimization, dehumanization, etc. from the DPSCS, and it got to the point that DPSCS headquarters blocked my cell phone from calling any jails or high-ranking individuals such as secretary of the state, etc.

The DPSCS equally started messing with my paycheck, hours, and denying me the opportunities that I was supposed to have on a normal day. DPSCS blackballed me from getting another job. Because of all these were happening to me, I wrote a letter to Governor Elijah on June, 18, 2018. And on June 19, 2018, I sent the governor the letter, pleading with him to come to my aid because of the discrimination and victimization DPSCS was given to me. On July 2, 2018, someone from the secretary of the state office pretended that he or she was trying to solve the issues by restating all the illegal treatments that I was undergoing in DPSCS without offering help or solutions. On July 6, 2018, at 6:08 p.m., I wrote a matter of record to the secretary of the state, asking him why he never offered a solution or an assistant to my ongoing victimization. I never received any response or answers to my questions.

When I got fed up trying to resolve my victimization, discrimination, bullying, harassment, being blackballed, and be a target in DPSCS, I reached out to the EEOC and placed discrimination charges against DPSCS. On July 31, 2018, I signed the EEOC discrimination charges paperwork with the impression that DPSCS would put an end to the victimizing and dehumanizing of me. Rather they came even harder on me. They tried everything to fire me from state service and destroy my life, just like they did to other Nigerians. While at CDF, and for the first time in my life working as a correctional officer, the former warden of CDF, Kathy, former assistant warden Tammy, and the current security chief treated me like a human being. I became the CDF DNA collector, got trained in traffic, OCMS. They gave me an opportunity and something to look up to as a reason to come to work. Some of the female officers at CDF started picking on me, saying that I'm trying to take their correctional officer boyfriends from them. They ganged up again, trying to make it seem like I don't get along with people. They also started to disclose my personal information to the CDF detainees. Some of the information they told the detainees was the type of handgun that I bring to work and store it in the master control just like every other officer.

It got to the point that I wrote a matter of record on October 21, 2018, to be transferred to the headquarters for safety reasons. Luckily for me, and with the help of Warden Kathy, I was able to get a job at the medical department as a project manager and statistic data analyst. I left CDF at the end of October and started working in my new position at the JI Building, not far from CDF, on November 2018. I was working under Chief Joseph. Both Chief Joseph and Warden Kathy agreed that I would be working on civilian clothing rather than uniform because of the nature of my duty. With the help of Chief Joseph and Deputy Commissioner Thomas, DPSCS headquarters was forced to unblock my phone number, create a DPSCS work e-mail for me, and set up a computer password for me. When I got to JI Building, Major Angela started harassing me and making racial comments toward me. She told me to stop dressing in civilian clothing that I have fewer years as a correctional officer. Before I knew what was happening, she created a situation whereby all the officers started picking on me. Major Angela made comments like "She's got to go," "This one is different," "She doesn't belong here" toward me every time she passed by my office. Officers at the commissioner's house believed that my type doesn't belong in the same group with them. Those officers tried everything to get Deputy Commissioner Thomas to send me back to the CDF, including telling him that I was crazy. Everything was going great, both working as the CDF DNA collector and running the medical sector as the project manager and statistic data analyst, until Major Angela, who has been trying to send me back to CDF, finally had me sent back to CDF on January 11, 2019, *after Warden Kathy and Assistant Warden Tammy retired. I tried explaining to the new warden, Warden Rebecca, about my condition; but she refused to reason with me. So I have requested to be transferred out since the matter of record that I wrote on October 21, 2018, was never acknowledged. Warden Rebecca sent me on another administrative leave with full pay on January 11, 2019, pending my transfer to the headquarters.*

While I was on administrative leave, Warden Rebecca, Miss Pamela (manager of employee relations unit), and other people from headquarters started harassing and threatening me that I would lose my job. These people were trying to force me into undergoing another medical evaluation so that they can fire me with a fake medical report. For the record, the state doctor lied in my medical report the first time and I knew he was going to lie again. On March 11, 2019, Warden Rebecca ganged up with Miss Pamela and attempted to fire me by introducing a fake employee's disciplinary mitigation conference at CDF. On April 22, 2019, I got another letter for a medical work evaluation appointment. On April 25, 2019, I went to Pivot Occupational Health, and Doctor Ghansham saw me. The state doctor told me that DPSCS said that I threatened a coworker in October 2018 but later changed it to January before I went on administrative leave. But all that were made-up lies just for them to use that avenue to fire me. And because of that, they are sending me to Pivot Occupational Health. DPSCS headquarters lied again to get me fired from state services. After the state doctor finished hearing my tale of the ongoing victimization from the DPSCS, alongside reviewing my medical history that my primary care doctor gave as evidence that I'm okay to return to work, Doctor Ghansham referred me to a psychological evaluation. Based on what he told me, Doctor Ghansham was requested by my agency to send me to IPE.

The state doctor wrote in his summary: "Stay in my current position, full report to follow." I went to the commissioner's house at the O'Brien House to report to Deputy Commissioner Thomas that DPSCS headquarters are trying to fire me from state service illegally through made-up lies against me. Deputy Commissioner Thomas was busy, so I left. On April 26, 2019, I received a letter from DPSCS saying that I am banned from entering O'Brien House, all the correctional facilities, and DPSCS buildings. As I anticipated, on May 2, 2019, the state medical doctor lied in my initial workability evaluation. He used the first fake medical records to restate his only report, saying that I have a borderline intelligence disorder based on the first doctor's IQ test. On May 21, 2019, DPSCS started cutting my paycheck. My check was from 80 hours in two weeks to 67.8 hours. When I asked the current warden of CDF, Warden Matthew, he informed me that Miss Pamela gave him an order for him to start using my leave hours while I am still on administrative leave that I was forced on me. On May 3, 2019, I went to another psychological evaluation conducted by Dr. Emma, a licensed psychologist. Sir, when my psychological report came back, the recommendation that Dr. Emma gave DPSCS was for them to keep me on the administrative leave and initiate psychotherapy for the depression, stress, and mood lability that I'm currently suffering, a result of the continuous work harassment that I encountered from 2015 till present.

She also told DPSCS in her report to move me to a different work location once I started responding well to the psychotherapy treatment. I was diagnosed with adjustment disorder with depressed mood and other specified trauma- and stressor-related disorder (work-related stress). On May 30, 2019, the final medical workability came out. State medical doctor wrote on his report that DPSCS should not give me any reasonable medical accommodation now or in thereby future and that based on his opinion, I should be fired from state service as a result of the medical condition that the department has caused me from 2015 to present. Doctor

Ghansham undermined the psychological and medical report that I start treatment and get my life back and went on creating more pain, stress, and depression for me by lying on my medical report so that I can get fired and lose all that I have ever worked for here in America. Mr. Ethan, it will interest you to know that almost all the state medical doctors that work for the DPSCS are lying on innocent correctional officers. Officers are illegally fired from state service as a result of the lies that state doctors make on their medical report. Sir, I will advise you to conduct a federal medical investigation on all DPSCS doctors and their role in producing false medical reports that have destroyed millions of correctional officers' lives.

Congressman, a lot of illegal activities are happening at the DPSCS that goes unreported. Please, sir, conduct federal investigations, and you will get a shock of your life on the level of corruption that goes on at the DPSCS. The most painful part of all this is that on June 4, 2019, DPSCS placed my picture and name in all the jails and prison in Maryland like I was a common criminal. Also, on June 5, 2019, I got a letter from DPSCS giving me options that countered the psychological medical recommendation of the doctor. Miss Pamela and other higher people in DPSCS are illegally trying to fire me and destroy my life. They gave me until June 13, 2019, to resign or I get fired. Please, Mr. Ethan, help me. You are my last hope. My dream of a better life is about to be destroyed by DPSCS.

On June 12, 2019, I responded to the DPSCS's demand to resign or get fired from the state service. In my letter, I told them that I would not resign and neither would I pick one out of the three options they gave me.

Correctional Officer II
Margaret Rose
Baltimore, MD 21214

Department of Public Safety and Correctional Services
Office of Secretary Human Resources Services Division
300 East Joppa Rd. Suite 100
Towson, Maryland 21286–3020

Responding to the State Medical Director's Unlawful
Medical Recommendation:

The State Medical Director Ghansham illegally provided
a false medical report, per DPSCS Human Resources
Division's request, to be used as a valid reason to force
me, Correctional Officer Margaret Rose, to resign or get
fired by the division. Most importantly, knowing the
victimization the DPSCS has subjected me to since 2015
to date and their three illegal attempts to dismiss me from
the state service, I at this moment move a motion to dismiss
DPSCS's unlawful actions against my employment with
overwhelming evidence. Notably, I, Correctional Officer
Margaret Rose, from a reasonable person's point of view, is
at this moment refusing to choose any of the options given
from the letter and also on the above date as a result of the
evidence that is beyond every reasonable doubt, which will
soon be brought to light. In addition to this, after reading
the state medical director's first and final workability
evaluation report, a psychological report that was conducted
by Doctor Jenkins, alongside with Dr. Mutsa Munjoma,
my primary care doctor's medical history, together with my
educational background in law enforcement and correctional
administration, criminal justice, forensic investigation,
homeland security and criminal justice master's degree and
also with my experience working in the medical field, being
a trained correctional officer, and working as an analyst who

has mastered the advance skill of detecting inconsistencies have all aided me in articulating and analyzing Doctor Ghansham's medical report and discovering that he intentionally lied on his medical report, undermining the medical oath he took as a doctor, which constitutes a medical misconduct and negligence in providing proper medical information that would have assisted me in receiving treatments. In the state medical director's final workability evaluation, he stated the following: "I also, referred Miss Margaret Rose for an IPE. Dr. Patricial Jenkins performed an IPE on May 14, 2019. She determined that based on this evaluation, Miss Margaret Rose is not psychologically able to perform the essential duties of her position. As yet she has not sufficiently resolved her emotional distress, feeling of persecution, and internalized trauma. She needs to remain on leave while she initiates counseling. Based on the medical records reviewed, history provided by Miss Margaret Rose, and on physical examination today, it is my opinion that Miss Margaret Rose is unable to safely, consistently, and reliably perform her essential job duties with or without reasonable accommodations in the near or foreseeable future." Additionally, Dr. Patricial Jenkins findings were as follows: "Personality structure is intact and reasonably well adjusted. She shows capacity for empathy concern for others, respect for the rights of others, close family ties, and positive outlook on life overall. Her current functioning is impacted by job related stress and worry. She internalized emotional trauma that impacts her moods and reactions to stressors. Based on this evaluation, Miss Margaret Rose is not psychologically able to perform the essential duties of her position as yet; she has not sufficiently resolved her emotional distress feelings of persecution and internalized trauma. She needs to remain on leave while she initiates counseling. She needs a therapeutic venue to process and resolve her feelings about her work situation before she resumes her duties. When she shows therapeutic progress in emotional resolution and ability to utilize effective strategies to manage stressors, she should be considered for a transfer to a different location. Her mental health and subsequently, her job performance will be compromised if she returns to the same work setting with exposure to recurring stressors."

She went further in her diagnostic impression and recommended the following:

F43-21: Adjustment disorder with depressed mood.

F43-8: Other specified trauma-and stressor-related disorder (work-related stress).

Recommendations:

It is recommended that Miss Margaret Rose remains on leave while she initiates psychotherapy and counseling. As she shows progress, she should be considered for return to work at a different location. Psychotherapy is recommended for depression, stress, and mood liability and to resolve feelings about her job situation. Miss Margaret Rose should participate in a weekly therapy session initially until she shows progress in resolving her emotional distress. A psychiatric evaluation is recommended for further assessment of symptoms and aid in determining if medication is appropriate. Consultation with her treatment providers is recommended to assess progress and determine when she should return to work.

In like manner, my primary care doctor, Mutsa Munjoma's medical workability evaluation and medical history made on April 24, 2019, stated: "No history of mental illness. No history of substance abuse. DPSCS Task Analysis of Employee: Patients doesn't require any work restrictions, patient's physical exam without abnormal findings; the patient is capable of performing her job. Functions: No restrictions."

Nonetheless, I will be attaching both the psychological medical report, the summary of three doctor's reports, together with the outcome that I'm requesting for as a result of my ongoing discrimination and victimization. Be advised that since 2015 till present DPSCS has been violating nonstop on my rights that is guaranteed in the Fourteenth Amendment, Section 1, of the United States Constitution. The Supreme Court granted me this right by saying, "Persons born or naturalized in the United States, and subject to the jurisdiction thereof, are citizens of the United States and the state wherein they reside. No state shall make or enforce any law which shall abridge the privileges or immunities of citizens of the United States; nor shall any state deprive any person of life, liberty, or property, without due process of law; nor deny to any person within its jurisdiction the equal protection of the laws." DPSCS is in violation. As for the right to receive medical treatment under the Fourteenth Amendment, the state doctor is in violation. And also the Eighth Amendment, which states that "the United States Constitution is the section of the Bill of Rights that states that that punishments must be fair, cannot be cruel or unusual punishment." Most importantly, DPSCS is violating Title VII of the Civil Rights Act of 1964, which declared a federal law that prohibits employers from discriminating against employees based on sex, race, color, national origin, and religion. Alongside with the annotated Code of Maryland, State Personnel and Pensions Article, Title 2, Section 2302; Title 4, Section 4-106; Title 5, Section 5-211, et seq.; Title 6, Section 6-102; and Title 11, Sections 11-104 and 11-105, the state of Maryland's policy in bullying in the workplace. This law became effective in January 1, 2017. Again, the state medical director committed fraud under the Eighth US Code § 1324c., penalties for document fraud.

DPSCS Office of the Secretary, Human Resources Services Division, I am under a federal protections act against retaliation, and you all violated it. Again, I at this moment move a motion to dismiss all the illegal attempts to fire me from state service. And if the motion is not granted, I, Correctional Officer Margaret Rose, will invoke the Subtitle 10 of the Correctional Officers' Bill of Rights and § 11-1008. Hearing/Cobra Rights as the alternative method of my hearing. Also, my COBRA board members will be from Igbo tribe in Nigeria. Important reminder: any interruption of payment, whether it's intentional or unintentional, will affect my basic human needs of food, shelter, clothing, and health care. This illegal action is known to be a violation of human rights.

Sincerely,

Her Royal Majesty, Princess Margaret Rose, Mouthpiece of Her People, the Second

Correctional Officer II, DNA Collector, Project Manager, Statistics Data Analyst, and Forensics Investigator

The reason for my refusal was because DPSCS was trying to intimidate me into resigning, which I wasn't having. Also, the department went against the medical advice of the psychologist that they forced on me. I stood my ground by saying, "Psych doctor said to remain on leave, get psychotherapy treatment for the long-term trauma caused by work-related stress, when showing progress come back to work and agency should transfer me to other job location."

On June 13, 2019, I received an e-mail from DPSCS human resources officer at 1:31 p.m. In the e-mail, she stated the following:

Good afternoon, Miss Margaret Rose: In order to honor your request (in part) we would like to meet with you here tomorrow, Friday, June 14, 2019, at 11:00 a.m. The location is Department of Public Safety and Correctional

Services. *Human Resources Services Division, 300 E Joppa Road, Suite 1000, Towson, MD 21286. Please reply by 5:00 p.m. today. Thank you.*

Human Resources Officer

Employee Health Service

On June 13, 2019, at 2:31 p.m., I responded to the above e-mail by saying, *"Good afternoon, I saw your e-mail, and I will be there tomorrow by 11:00 a.m."* I went to the DPSCS headquarters on June 14, 2019. When I got there, the human resources officer and people from the employee health service offered and scheduled me for a psychotherapy that was recommended by Dr. Emma through the Employee Assistant Program (EAP). On June 18, 2019, at approximately 11:00 a.m., I went for my first psychotherapy treatment. According to the therapist, I had two more sessions left. The therapist made another therapy appointment for June 27, 2019. We both agreed that my next appointment would be held after the second session of the psych therapy treatment. Unfortunately, DPSCS deprived me the right to receive the full medical assistance as was requested by the licensed psychologist Dr. Emma.

On the same June 18, 2019, I received an e-mail from the CDF warden, Warden Matthew. Through his e-mail, he informed me to report to the DPSCS headquarters on June 20, 2019, for another mitigation conference. DPSCS didn't see any other day to put the conference but on my birthday.

On June 20, 2019, I went to the mitigation conference as ordered. When I got there, Miss Pamela was at it again, forcing me to believe and say that I have a disability and because of it I'm unfit to work as a correctional officer now or in the future. My response to her was, "No, can't do. Nothing is wrong with me, and I can work." Miss Pamela tried intimidating me to go on medical leave without pay. I again objected to her demands. Miss Pamela threatened to fire me if I didn't resign, accept that I have a medical disability and thus unfit to be a correctional officer, or go on medical leave without pay. I still stood my ground. I told Miss Pamela that I was supposed to be in psychotherapy because of my job-related long-term internalized trauma and depressed mood. As I was trying to explain further, Miss Pamela ordered me to shut up and not to speak again. I in return said to her, "It's under my First Amendment right to express myself." Miss Pamela said, "Well, your First Amendment right has limitation while you are on the state property." As I was debating with Miss Pamela, the armed security officer that headquarters placed to watch all my moves instructed me to keep my voice down. When I couldn't stand Miss Pamela's best bullshit, her feelings, and her attitude, I left the conference meeting. Before I walked out, I told her, "Miss Pamela, do your job. Illegally fire me if you want, because I will never say that I have a disability or unfit to be a correctional officer." On my way out, Miss Pamela responded, "You gave me no other choice."

Another thing that DPSCS did to hurt my feelings, which I know they don't particularly care for, was that anytime headquarters orders me to come to a meeting, upon getting there, armed security officers would come out and start searching my bag, asking me if I had a gun. Not only that, one of the armed security officers would follow me around, from and to the meeting. DPSCS headquarters posted my image all over the department as if I was a high-profile terrorist, and they treated me as one.

On June 22, 2019, at approximately 10:15 a.m., I got a notice of termination letter from the headquarters, addressed to me through the US Postal Service. I was fired on the weekend of my birthday.

There was one funny thing that happened throughout my illegal termination process. The DPSCS headquarters couldn't express themselves in a grammatically correct way in their report against me. All they did was copy back the letter that I sent them and made it look like it was their idea. Dumb as there all are, they would give me back the letter that I wrote to them but in the form of them writing the letter to me, thinking that I wouldn't find out that they stole the words that I wrote in my letter and just gave it back to me to sign. In one instance of them copying my letter, changing a few words, and giving it back to me, I got upset and I said to them, "What do you people think that y'all are doing? Like for real, what? Is this one of your sick jokes? Do I look retarded? That I am an African doesn't mean that I'm stupid.

Why would you people insult my intelligence by taking the letter that I sent to you all and turn it around to look like it was y'all that wrote it and then expect me to read and sign the same paper that I sent to you people? The only difference is the DPSCS letterhead. Why should I reread a paper that I wrote in the first place and gave to you so you all can address the ongoing issues? I have invested a lot of my time acquiring this knowledge, so don't insult my intelligence. Changing my letters to fit your reality and then giving them back to me to sign so you could send them over to your so-called leaders, making me look like I am causing the problem in the department. That's ridiculous, with all due respect, where did you people get your degrees from? Was it ordered from the Amazon? Or was it bought at the Dollar Store? Buy one get one free. Could it be at the Rainbow Store? Buy one get one half off the price. It must be from Walmart then, two for $3.99? The reason why am asking is that a reasonable person that went to school and got her degree knows that copying another person's idea without giving credit is known as plagiarism. So technically you are plagiarizing my letters and then turning them around for me to sign it. That's dumb."

Before I got terminated, I reached out to the Maryland Commission on Civil Rights for assistance. I filed charges against DPSCS. After I got terminated, I also went back to the office of the Commission on Civil Rights, and they amended the charges so as to include medical mislabeling and unlawful termination. Maryland Commission on Civil Rights scheduled a fact-finding conference between DPSCS and me at their office on August 15, 2019. Knowing that every boss has a boss, I went to Annapolis, Maryland, to speak to the state governor. When I got there, I was informed that the governor wasn't available. On July 9, 2019, I sent another letter to Annapolis and addressed it to the governor. I never heard back from the governor, but that didn't stop me from getting my documentation, nor did it deter me from preparing for my case against DPSCS on August.

July 9, 2019
Mr. Elijah,

The Department of Public Safety and Correctional Services retaliated back by illegally terminating my employment as a result of the letter I wrote to you last year.

Mr. Governor, after I wrote to you last year about the discrimination, dehumanization, bullying, harassment, false medical documentation, being socially disenfranchised, abuse of power from the department headquarters, denying of the job opportunity, death threat that was made on my life, etc. Sir, I will attach the copy of the 2018 letter to you alongside with other documents so that you can understand the recurring issues at the DPSCS. Mr. Elijah, after writing to you, DPSCS got a hold of the letter and increased the level of the unfair treatment that I initially encountered. Sir, the 2018 issue that I brought to your attention was never solved, rather my situation at work got worse. Also, Miss Nicole, who happened to be the associate manager at the Office of the Secretary, restated back the issues that I was having but never offered any solution, assistance, or suggestion. I wrote Miss Nicole a matter of record asking why she never assisted me or solved my problems. Miss Nicole never responded to the matter of record that I wrote to her last year, July 6, 2018, at approximately 6:08 p.m.

Governor, that wasn't the only thing that happened to me after I wrote to you. The DPSCS blocked my cell phone number from calling high-ranking people like secretary of the state and others. DPSCS headquarters blackballed me from getting another job in and outside the state agency. Headquarters intentionally interfered with my leave time by reducing both my personal, sick, and annual leaves while I was still coming to work. Also, they decreased my pay rate while other correctional officers were getting increases. Headquarters tried everything to frustrate me into resigning, but I never did. Some supervisors and officers who were not familiar with my case or knew what I went through joined them as well, just so I could be illegally fired from the state service. Officers were calling me crazy, female officers were accusing me of trying to take their correctional officer boyfriends from them, other female officers were accusing me of having sex with male officers while the rest of DPSCS officers, supervisors, headquarters, and administrators saw me as a snitch.

Mr. Governor, in the middle of all this, former warden of Chesapeake Detention Facility, Warden Kathy; Assistant Warden Tammy; and current security chief all gave me the opportunity of being trained in the areas of DNA collection, traffic officer, OCMS, etc. These great leaders gave a nobody like me a reason to come to work. Nevertheless, some of the female officers at CDF ganged up again, trying to make it seem like I have issues getting along with people. They also started disclosing my personal information to the detainees. Some of the information they told the detainees was the type of handgun that I bring to work and that I store it in the master control center just like every other officer. I wrote a matter of record on October 21, 2018, to be transferred to the headquarters for safety reasons but never got the transfer that I requested. Luckily for me, with the help of the former warden, Miss Kathy, I was able to get a job at the medical department as a project manager and statistic data analyst to assist with the medical settlement agreement that is currently going on now. I left CDF at the end of October and started working in my new position at the JI Building in November 2018. I was working under Chief Joseph. Both Chief Joseph and Warden Kathy agreed that I should dress in civilian clothing rather than uniform because of the nature of my duty.

With the help of Chief Joseph and Deputy Commissioner Thomas, DPSCS headquarters was forced to unblock my phone number, create a DPSCS work e-mail for me, and set up a computer password for me. When I got to the JI

Building, Major Angela started harassing me and making racial comments toward me. She told me to stop dressing in civilian clothing because I have less years as a correctional officer. Unsurprisingly, before I knew what was happening, Major Angela created a situation whereby all the officers started picking on me. Major Angela made comments like "She's got to go," "This one is different," "She doesn't belong here" anytime she passes by my office. Officers at the commissioner's house believed that my type doesn't belong in the same group with them or to work with high-ranking people. Those officers tried everything to poison both Chief Joseph's and Deputy Commissioner Thomas's minds for them to send me back to CDF. These officers at the commissioner's house went as far as telling Deputy Commissioner Thomas that I was crazy. Unfortunately for me, Major Angela and the other officers at the commissioner's house created a situation because they saw me in civilian clothing. Mr. Governor, for me to give peace a chance, I went back wearing uniform while still working under Chief Joseph and Deputy Commissioner Thomas. I was still working as the CDF DNA collector and running the medical sector as the project manager and statistic data analyst until Major Angela, who has been trying to send me back to CDF, finally had her way and sent me back to CDF on January 11, 2019. This was after Warden Kathy and Assistant Warden Tammy retired.

When I got to CDF, I tried explaining to the new warden, Warden Rebecca, about my condition. She refused to reason with me. Because of her inability to understand my situation, I requested for her to transfer me out in a matter of record that I wrote on October 21, 2018. But it was never acknowledged. Warden Rebecca, during her first time in meeting me, sent me home on another administrative leave with full pay on January 11, 2019, pending my transfer to the headquarters. Mr. Governor, when I was on administrative leave, Warden Rebecca; Miss Pamela, manager of employee relations unit; and other people from headquarters started *harassing and threatening me that I would lose my job. These people forced me to undergo another medical evaluation so that they can fire me with a false medical report. For the record, the state doctor lied on my medical report the first time and I knew he was going to lie again. On March 11, 2019, Warden Pachelo ganged up with Miss Pamela and attempted to fire me through introducing a false employee's disciplinary mitigation conference at CDF.*

On April 22, 2019, I got another letter for a medical work evaluation appointment. On April 25, 2019, I went to Pivot Occupational Health, and Doctor Ghansham saw me. The state doctor told me that the DPSCS said that I threatened a coworker in October 2018, but later changed it to January, before I went on administrative leave. But all that was a made-up lie. It was just an avenue for them to fire me. And because of that, they sent me to Pivot Occupational Health. Again, DPSCS headquarters lied to get me fired from state service. But after the state doctor heard my side of the story about the ongoing victimization from the DPSCS, alongside with reviewing my medical history that my primary care doctor gave me as evidence to show that I'm okay to return to work, Doctor Ghansham referred me to a psychological evaluation. Doctor Ghansham informed me that my agency, which is DPSCS, requested that he send me to another IPE. The state doctor wrote in his summary, saying, "Stay in my current position, full report to follow." I went to the commissioner's house in O'Brien House to report to Deputy Commissioner Thomas that DPSCS headquarters is trying to fire me from state service illegally through made-up lies. Unfortunately, Deputy Commissioner Thomas was busy, so I left. On April 26, 2019, I received a letter from DPSCS saying that I am banned from entering O'Brien House, all the correctional facilities, and DPSCS buildings.

As I anticipated, on May 2, 2019, the state medical doctor lied on my initial workability evaluation. He used the first false medical records to restate in his report. Doctor

Ghansham stated that I have a borderline intelligence disorder based on the first doctor's IQ test. On May 21, 2019, DPSCS began to reduce my paycheck. My check was from 80 hours in two weeks to 67.8 hours. When I asked the current warden of CDF, Warden Matthew, he informed me that Miss Pamela gave him an order for him to start using my leave hours while I am still on administrative leave that was forced on me. On May 3, 2019, I went to another psychological evaluation conducted by Dr. Emma, a licensed psychologist. Mr. Governor, it will interest you to know that when my psychological report came back, the recommendation that Dr. Emma gave DPSCS was for them to keep me on the administrative leave and initiate psychotherapy for the depression, stress, and mood lability that I'm currently suffering from as a result of the continuous work harassment that I have encountered from 2015 till present. Dr. Emma also told DPSCS in her report to move me to a different work location once I start responding well to the psychotherapy treatment. I was diagnosed with adjustment disorder with depressed mood and other specified trauma-and stressor-related disorder (work-related stress).

On May 30, 2019, the final medical workability came out. State medical doctor, Dr. Ghansham, wrote in his report that DPSCS should not give me any reasonable medical accommodation now or in nearby future. And based on his opinion, I should be fired. Doctor Ghansham undermined the psychological and medical report that I start psychotherapy treatment and get my life back and went on creating more pain, stress, and depression for me by lying on the medical report. Mr. Governor, it will interest you again to know that almost all the state medical doctors that work for the DPSCS are lying on innocent correctional officers. Officers are illegally getting fired from state service as a result of the lies the state doctors make on their medical reports. Sir, I will advise you to conduct a federal medical investigation on all the DPSCS doctors and the role they play in producing false *medical reports that have destroyed millions of correctional officers' lives. Governor Elijah, a lot of illicit activities are happening at the DPSCS that goes unreported. Please, sir, conduct a federal investigation, and you will get the shock of your life on the level of corruption that goes on at the DPSCS.*

The most painful part of all this is that on June 4, 2019, DPSCS placed my picture and name in all the jails and prison in Maryland like I was a common criminal. Also, on June 5, 2019, I got a letter from DPSCS giving me options that countered the psychological medical recommendation made by the doctor. Miss Pamela and other higher people in DPSCS illegally tried to fire me and destroy my life. They gave me until June 13, 2019, to resign, agree that I have medical issues, or get fired. However, I wrote back to DPSCS informing them that I will not resign, neither will I agree that I have a medical problem. Governor, I wrote to the United State congressman Elijah Cummings explaining to him about the ongoing victimization from the DPSCS. Mr. Cummings contacted DPSCS on my behalf, but Miss Pamela and the others at the headquarters refused to reason with the United States House representative. Mr. Elijah, DPSCS referred me to the EAP program. Sir, I went to the EAP section, but I was supposed to go back another two more sections. Unfortunately, again, Miss Pamela denied me the opportunity of getting the medical treatment that I needed. On June 18, 2019, I received another letter for a mitigation conference. When I got there, Governor, Miss Pamela forced me to believe that I'm medically sick and can't work again. She equally tried forcing me into going on a medical leave of absence without pay. Sir, I told her no, that she should send me back to therapy so that I can complete my treatment and that the department should transfer me to another location based on Dr. Emma's recommendation.

Mr. Governor, it will surprise you to know that the DPSCS sent me a notice of termination through the United

States Postal Services on June 22, 2019. Again, Governor, it's no longer news to you that the DPSCS is corrupt. With all due respect, Mr. Governor, the system is corrupt and needs to be replaced. People like Miss Pamela, Major Angela, and others have corrupted the system. Governor, do something. Innocent people like me are suffering because I refused to be part of the corrupt system. Sir, the so-called leaders you placed at the DPSCS don't seem like they are doing a great job, because if there are, how come I got fired rather than attending the psychotherapy? Mr. Larry, do you know that DPSCS discriminates immigrants and they target Nigerian correctional officers to which I'm a victim of. Sir, it's painful for me to see that every time I visit the DPSCS headquarters no immigrants are working there. Mr. Governor, DPSCS is supposed to be a culturally diverse division, correct? But presently, sir, they are culturally biased. Mr. Elijah, DPSCS is corrupt. Mr. Elijah, DPSCS supposed to treat its employees fairly, firmly, and impartially but correctional officers are suffering. Sir, please force DPSCS to give immigrant correctional officers and other immigrants an opportunity. Tell them to stop treating us like we have no business coming to America for a better life.

Sir, immigrants at the DPSCS are suffering. We need opportunities just like the Americans. Sir, immigrant correctional officers are also human beings. Please help us, Governor. DPSCS headquarters is running the division as if we are all in a third world country. Governor, DPSCS is corrupt. Do something. Mr. Elijah, please, with your executive power as the governor of the state of Maryland and one of the leaders of the free world country, America, please command DPSCS to give me back my job, send me to therapy, pay me, and relocate me to a different jobsite. Mr. Governor, this Wednesday is pay day, and I don't know how I will be able to pay my house rent and food and meet up with my other basic human needs. Mr. Elijah, please use your executive power to inform DPSCS to continue *paying me until I return to work just like the psychologist Dr. Emma recommended. Sir, I'm about to lose my apartment and become homeless all because of the corruption that goes unreported at the department. Governor, I know that you have the manpower and the resources to help me. Please assist me. I'm innocent, and I haven't committed any crime, other than being an immigrant working in a racist department. Sir, I have attached all my documents.*

Before I forget, Mr. Elijah, I will like for you to know that DPSCS changed all the current and previous issues to fit their version of reality by making it appear that I am the unfortunate person who is creating problems in the division. Rather than solve the ongoing issues, DPSCS used this approach. This approach was effective as a result of the information that I shared with them through my writing. Instead of DPSCS solving my problems or better yet create lies to cover up the four going to five years of victimization that I suffered from, they chose to steal my ideas and made it theirs, thinking that I will not find out. Mr. Governor, DPSCS headquarters people cannot articulate appropriately in their writings, and that's why they kept taking my ideas and making it as theirs. Sir, a lot of people who are working at the headquarters are not qualified to be there. DPSCS does their hiring process on who-you-know basis rather than what you know. Sir, please put some of the immigrants at the headquarters and watch how DPSCS will transform from a corrupt to a non-corrupt system. Governor, please do something to help me because this is my second time writing to you over the same ongoing victimization.

Yours sincerely,
Margaret Rose

Knowing that I was only one person going after the entire department without a lawyer or union representative, it motivated me to study and master my case very well. Buying time while waiting for the Civil

Rights Commission's fact-findings conference to happen, I applied for unemployment, food stamp, cash assistance, and free medical assistance. Also, knowing that the state medical director lied on my medical report that resulted in my illegal termination made me reach out to him so that he can sign my medical disability benefits form that was sent to me by Transamerica Insurance. I also gave DPSCS their copy to fill out too. Since both the state doctor and headquarters enjoy lying to people, I gave them something to lie about and to show them that I know the game they are playing. As I anticipated, the state doctor refused to sign my paperwork. He turned around and said, "You signed no patient-and-doctor relationship." The response that I gave him was, "Sir, you must sign my disability paperwork for me so that I can go and get free money from my insurance, since you and DPSCS lied on my medical report saying that I was medically disabled. Please sign my paperwork because I will be coming to your office so that you can sign the paperwork or you return me to work since we all know that you lied on me."

On July 16, 2019, at approximately 9:45 a.m., my unemployment phone interview was conducted. During the interview, the lady informed me that the interview is being recorded, which was okay with me. During the interview, the unemployment office woman asked me what happened and why was I fired. I told her the whole story. Afterward, she asked if I was ready and willing to work. The responded that I gave her was, "Yes, I'm willing and ready to work anytime. Nothing is wrong with me. DPSCS and their doctor lied on me just for me to get fired." At the end of the interview, the lady advised me that she will get in contact with DPSCS and after that I will be qualified for the unemployment benefits because she didn't see anything that I did wrong. On July 29, 2019, I received a mail from the state of Maryland Department of Labor, Licensing and Regulation Division of Unemployment Insurance. My claim was discharged. The determination was made on July 26, 2019, based on section 8-1003. The unemployment discharged notification stated the following: "Metropolitan transition CTR discharged the claimant on 06/22/2019 because the employer felt that the claimant was not able and available for work. Insufficient evidence has been presented to show any misconduct in connection with the work. As a result, the circumstances surrounding the separation do not warrant disqualification under section 8-1002 or 8-1003 of the Maryland unemployment insurance law. Benefits are allowed. If otherwise eligible."

Upon receiving this mail, I called the unemployment to know why my claim was discharged. The man who picked up the phone told me that I stated during my phone interview that I wasn't ready and available to work. That was a big lie. I requested the copy of their findings so I could make sense of what the man was saying on the phone. The copy of the unemployment findings was mailed to me on August 6, 2019. Lo and behold, when I went through the finding's paperwork, I discovered that the answers that I gave on the phone during the interview weren't the same thing written on the paper.

Somebody changed all the answers that I gave, and because of that, the unemployment office discharged my claim. Determined to find the truth and the reason why I was denied unemployment drove me into calling the unemployment office. I informed the woman who I spoke to on the phone that the answers I gave on the phone during my unemployment phone interview got compromised because the answers to the questions that I saw in the paperwork didn't reflect what I said on the phone. I also told her that because of the changes that were made on the fact-finding paperwork, I was denied unemployment insurance. The woman, on the other hand, didn't even care; so I dropped the phone. That was how I was denied unemployment payment.

Similarly, the Maryland Department of Human Services denied me the food stamp assistance because the state medical doctor never signed the paperwork when all the while he was the one that labeled me medically disabled and unfit for duty. The DPSCS state doctor refused to sign the paper because he knew that I'm medically fine and nothing was wrong with me. I tried giving the same paperwork to my primary care doctor. She told me that she couldn't sign it because medically there is nothing wrong with me and that I can work. I wasn't mad at her because, in reality, I wasn't ill and I am not disabled. I can work. That again was how I lost the food stamp/cash assistance. I equally lost the Transamerica disability insurance benefit that I have faithfully paid throughout my career as a correctional officer.

In conclusion, that was how I lost everything that I have ever worked for since I came to America. My current status now includes, but are not limited to, no health insurance, life insurance, state benefits, source of income, job, government assistance, loss of my apartment, have an outstanding $60,000 student loan to pay back, and sleeping on my father's couch. I lost it all.

In the final analysis, these were the reasons DPSCS gave for terminating me. The first cause of termination, when asked to specify the rules violation and the incidents of violations with appropriate dates, DPSCS responded: "Disciplinary history." There was no disciplinary history during the reckoning period. My question is, why was I terminated since I didn't violate any rules or made any other violation incident? Furthermore, another cause for termination that the department gave was, "After one year of satisfactory employment as a correctional officer I, Miss Margaret Rose received a noncompetitive promotion to the position of correctional officer II. During her tenure at the DPSCS, Miss Margaret Rose's overall history of performance has met acceptable standards for an employee of her rank and classification." The next cause for termination based on my notice of termination by the department was, "Deputy Commissioner requested that employee health services schedule an appointment for her to be evaluated by the state medical director. She was crying at the commissioner's house on January 11, 2019; Deputy Commissioner ordered she be placed on administrative leave pending evaluation. And because she owned a gun."

Another question that I have for DPSCS was why did manager for employee relation take me off the administrative leave after my initial visit to the state doctor? The order that was given was for me to remain on leave until after the evaluation. Come to think of it, the only rule that I violated was that I began breathing hard, holding my stomach, and crying and that I owned a gun. Please note that I wasn't combative, nor displaying any threatening or violent behavior. The only crime that I committed that made DPSCS fire me was that I was crying, holding my stomach, and breathing hard. My handgun was legal, and it's under my constitutional right to bear arms, Second Amendment to be exact. The department indirectly called me a terrorist when they made this comment: "Because she owned a gun." Significantly, the explanation the

DPSCS gave for terminating me from state service is as follows: "Based on the findings of Doctor Ghansham, Miss Margaret Rose cannot perform the essential duties of her position now or in the unforeseeable future." Hold it. Question, DPSCS. Where did your state doctor get his findings from? Because I know that it wasn't from the psychologist, and I know too well that my primary care doctor never said that in her medical report. Another explanation DPSCS headquarters provides: "Moreover, Doctor Ghansham has concluded that she is not suited for employment in a correctional environment." Oh my God, who employed these amateurs to work at headquarters? "Not suited for employment in a correctional environment." That right there is 100 percent gender discrimination. I have worked in the prison facilities, starting from prerelease jail and ending in a federal maximum-security detention facility. Like what the hell. Who wrote this termination letter? What is DPSCS talking about? I'm one of the best correctional officers that ever worked in DPSCS. The final explanation DPSCS gave was, "Finally, given the department's interest in protecting health, safety, and welfare of the employee, the department believes that Correctional Officer II Margaret Rose's separation of state services is the appropriate administrative action under the circumstances." Again, DPSCS indirectly accused me of being a violent person who posed a threat to the department. Under what circumstances? Why did I get disciplined when I never committed any crime, violated the rules, or have incident violations?

I couldn't wait to showcase my skills and beat DPSCS again in their game at the office of the Commission on Civil Rights. Knowing that I was one person going against the department of corruption, I went and brought out all the strategic methods that I gained and mastered throughout my educational journey as an associate degree holder in law enforcement and correctional administration, as bachelor's degree holder in criminal justice and forensic investigation, and a master's degree holder in homeland security and criminal justice. I wasn't only getting ready to combat DPSCS with my academic knowledge alone. I further employed the spiritual aspect of it. I was praying, fasting, meditating, covering myself with the blood of Jesus, and sending Holy Ghost fire to the DPSCS headquarters.

After binding and casting the department, soaking myself with the blood of Jesus, and using Holy Ghost's fire back to the sender and never to return on DPSCS, I was more than ready to attend the meeting on August 15, 2019. When I got to the office of the Commission on Civil Rights that was in downtown Baltimore, St. Paul Street, on August 15, 2019, I saw the person who was representing the department. DPSCS sent one of their top-notch EEO investigator who has a lot of experience in civil rights and discrimination battle. Without feeling intimidated, I stood up from where I was sitting, walked up to him, and shook his hands. Afterward, I looked into his eyes and asked him this question: "Oh, so you are the person the department sent to come a represent them." His response was, "Yes, I am. I see you have a lot of paperwork." I told him, "Yep, something like that." The commission's civil rights investigator came out and took us inside a conference room. When we got there, he offered us a seat, and afterward, he explained the legal process by which the fact-findings conference would be operating on. The civil rights investigator read the charges that I brought against the DPSCS. When finished, he opened the floor for questions and answers and objecting to any statement that seemed untrue. For me, it was the moment that I have been waiting for. I said in my mind, *It's show time, babe.*

The first question thrown to me by the civil rights investigator was, I believe, he asked me to explain what happened and why I felt like I was discriminated against by the department. In responding to his question, I gave him a download of what happened. I included the time, date, and people who did what to me; the post that I was assigned when they did what they did to me; the supervisors whom I reported the incident to; the names of supervisors who did their job and the ones who didn't; and the name of the others that ganged up with the officers. Meanwhile, the DPSCS's fancy EEO investigator was taking notes while I was talking. When I finished, the EEO man asked a question to me and I replied, giving him dates, time, place, and names of the concerned individuals. The civil rights investigator asked the EEO investigator why I was terminated, the EEO man response was, "While the department doesn't have a reasonable accommodation to offer Miss Margaret Rose, the state doctor said that we should give her no reasonable accommodation now or unforeseeable future, so the department had to decide to terminate her from the state service. Miss Margaret Rose wanted to work at headquarters; she can't get along with the other officers. We have moved her to three different jails; she kept having problems with the officers. I believed at some point she received a death threat, and after that, she wanted to work at headquarters. Officers were complaining about her; they said that she makes them feel uncomfortable and that her personality is intimidating. Am not sure if the case was investigated before the termination, and the reason why armed security officers follow her around is that she owned a gun."

I noticed something when the DPSCS's EEO investigator was talking, and I used it to my advantage. The man was reading out the whole thing from a paper. Like who does that? Well, I guess, DPSCS. Anyway, the civil rights man asked the EEO representative if I requested for a reasonable accommodation. His response was, "No, she didn't." Then the civil rights man asked why she was terminated if she never requested for a reasonable accommodation. The EEO man responded again, "Am not too sure why." As soon as he said that, I looked over his paper and found that the answer for that question wasn't written down for him. Right then my mind told me, *Miss. Margaret, go hard on him, slider DPSCS, and show no mercy.* I ask permission from the civil rights investigator if I could ask the EEO investigator questions because that's part of the rules of the conference. He okayed my turn to question the EEO man. The first question that I asked the EEO investigator was, "Sir, you said that officers were complaining that they don't feel comfortable around me because of my personality and that they feel intimidated around me? So who are these officers that accused me of intimidating them with my personality? Sir, the officers said that I intimidate them, not that I threatened them. Again, is it my fault that the officers felt intimidated about my personality? Basically, DPSCS fired me because their officers felt my presence was intimidating them and that I behave differently from everybody else. Why should I be fired because I don't behave like other officers, sir? Does that mean because I'm not corrupt, I don't sleep with top-ranked officials to get a promotion. You said that the armed security officers in which DPSCS ordered them to be following me around like I was a terrorist was as a result of me owning a gun? Am I the only correctional officer in DPSCS that has a registered gun? I obtained my handgun permission from the Maryland State Troopers. Do you think that the Troopers would have given me the handgun permit if they believed that I was incompetent? Just in case if you don't know, there is no such thing as 'no reasonable accommodation now or in an unforeseeable future.'"

After I completed my questions, the civil rights investigator asked me why I was moved to three different jails. My response to that question was, "Sir, on May 30, 2017, an ex-inmate of BCCC attacked me. Police were called. DPSCS IIU came. They promised to come back to solve my case, but they never did. Here is the police report. Officers were harassing and bullying me. I reported they ganged up against me. I reported a female officer flirting with an inmate. After the report, the officer and her friends came after me. I reported to all the supervisors at BCCC. Nobody did anything about it. On December 19, 2017, officers made a death threat on my life and put the paper in Major Brian's mailbox in the administrative area where inmates don't have any access, only case managers and officers. Supervisors joined the female officers to harass and bully me after I refused to sign my life away to waver liability off the state of Maryland when they finally kill me. I was eating spoilt food at work and wasn't allowed to attend officers' roll calls. A captain gave the order. Because of the pain I suffered, I came to EEO headquarters on January 12, 2018, for them to help me. I was told that they wouldn't be able to assist, that I should call IIU. When I called IIU on January 12, 2018, a lady in the Internal Investigation Unit of DPSCS told me that IIU doesn't investigate a death threat, but only after it happens. Then on January 31, 2018, I passed out while at work. I woke up and found myself in the hospital. On February 15, 2018, I passed out again, were crying inside the MRDCC jail, woke up, and found myself in the hospital. DPSCS framed me up that I'm crazy. Their state doctor said that I reason like a five grader." I was going on and on, nonstop.

As I was telling them the reason why DPSCS moved me to three different jails, I was also showing him the paperwork for each incident. The civil rights investigator asked the EEO investigator if he knows anything about the incidents that I listed, his response was, "No, I'm not aware of it." From the sincerity that came from his voice and his facial expression, I could tell that the DPSCS EEO investigator wasn't properly informed or equipped by the daughters of Jezebels that work at the department headquarters on the details of my case and the extent of damage that they sent him to clean up.

At that point, I was separated from the EEO investigator. I didn't know what the civil rights man told him or what they talked about. The only thing that I told the civil rights investigator was because of my generosity, I will get one million dollars from DPSCS for settlement after putting me through hell. The investigator informed me that he would look over the documentation that I brought to the fact-finding conference. After that, he will schedule another meeting for both parties to attend. I haven't heard from the Commission on Civil Rights.

Certainly, the DPSCS has created a negative impact and a stain on my life, career, and future that will never go away. The department tarnished my future employment opportunities in criminal justice after all the hard work and many years I have invested in myself.

These are some of the never-changing stains on my life that the department has caused me: I will never be able to work for the state of Maryland again as a result of this illegal termination. Secondly, my future has been altered and my employment market value has been depreciated. Third, I now have a health issue of depressed mood and internalize trauma of work-related stress. Next, my character has been defamed. I lost everything that I have worked so hard for. No job, no income, no benefits, and with $60,000 student loan to pay back. The DPSCS terminating my employment from state service wasn't because I was a dirty officer, or even that I violated any of their rules. To this following or that I violated any of their rules. However, I was terminated because they believe that my type was unsuited for employment in a correctional environment. I never knew that being an honest person with a moral conscience and ethics was a rule violation and punishable by termination at the DPSCS. The department fired me because they saw my personality to be intimidating. They know that I knew too much about their corrupt system and will one day expose them. The DPSCS headquarters saw me as a threat to their positions. They were scared of me because they saw me as a mysterious woman who can never be puzzled. It was terrifying for them to see a nobody like me standing up and challenging them and who was never afraid or intimidated by them. Headquarters saw me as competition to their current positions and were afraid and jealous. DPSCS headquarters believed that I would come after their positions at the headquarters, and that was why they all ganged up on me with the support of the so-called DPSCS leaders, and so they illegally fired me. I got fired because I did not exchange sex for positions or protection. I was never a corrupt officer. DPSCS knew that I would never compromise. That was why they fired me, because they are looking for people who would compromise. What happened to me at the DPSCS should never have happened in the first place, but because headquarters has gotten comfortable hurting, framing, and destroying correctional officers' lives, they believe that it's a normal thing to do to intimidate and punish an innocent person as well as discriminating, victimizing, and dehumanizing another human being.

DPSCS doesn't know how to fight a fair fight for two reasons: One is that almost everyone who occupied the positions at headquarters are inadequate, but like they said, "The only way to get to the top in DPSCS is to physically get on top of someone who mattered in the department." It's also known as "fuck your way into the system." They said that. I am just repeating what they said. The second one is that they are always at fault, but they are too arrogant and proud to say, "We are sorry for the misunderstanding." Instead of saying sorry, they turn around and utilize the method of fear, corruption, intimidation, discrimination, victimization, dehumanization, blackballing, ganging up, framing up, assassination, defamation of character, and using government influence to overpower poor, innocent correctional officers.

One thing people say that drives me crazy is, "Miss Margaret Rose, you know that you can't fight the government." Correctional officers and other people at the DPSCS are afraid of the headquarters and their leaders because they have been brainwashed. A true leader doesn't lead his or her people with fear, corruption, or assassination. Leaders lead their subjects with respect, integrity, humility, and love. DPSCS leads their people with fear, and that right there is not a characteristic of a leader. While waiting for the Civil Right Commission to get back to me, I have questions to ask DPSCS:

1. Why did you all pick me to victimize from 2015 to 2019? Why me?
2. How do you all pick your targets to victimize?
3. Do you people sleep well at night, after causing pain to innocent and helpless people and framing officers up to go to jail? How do you people do that, I mean, hurt people?
4. Why was my termination letter signed on June 20, 2019, the same day I was called for the mitigation conference and two days before I got terminated?
5. Why was I taken off from the administrative leave after my first visit to the state doctor but the order that was given stated after the end of medical evaluation?
6. Why do you people pay your doctors and psychological doctors to lie on the correctional officers' medical reports just for them to get fired?
7. Why were my pictures placed on every entering and exit post in all the Baltimore Downtown Jails on June 4, 2019, while I was still a correctional officer as of that time but later got terminated on June 22, 2019?
8. What was the main reason for my illegal termination? Is it because the department fears the light that I shine in the dark?
9. Why are you people after my life?
10. Where did the state doctor get his findings from, which made him believe that I was unfit for duty?
11. When would you people inform those officers that were illegally terminated as a result of a false medical report that those results were made up to get them fired?
12. Also, would you all ever going to let the world know that all the correctional officers who are currently serving time inside the prison facilities or about to get indicted are innocent of the crime they were accused of? Like when?
13. Finally, why is the department so corrupt? Why can't we do the right thing and care for each other, irrespective of our race, national origin, color, cultural background, ethnicity, language differences? And for heaven's sake, why can we all get along? What are we all fighting against each other for? It's not that serious?

www.ingramcontent.com/pod-product-compliance
Lightning Source LLC
Chambersburg PA
CBHW060602210326
41519CB00014B/3551